Charles Bradlaugh

Taxation

How it Originated, how it Is Spent and who Bears It. Second Edition

Charles Bradlaugh

Taxation

How it Originated, how it Is Spent and who Bears It. Second Edition

ISBN/EAN: 9783337476168

Printed in Europe, USA, Canada, Australia, Japan

Cover: Foto ©Suzi / pixelio.de

More available books at **www.hansebooks.com**

TAXATION:

HOW IT ORIGINATED, HOW IT IS SPENT,
AND WHO BEARS IT.

BY

CHARLES BRADLAUGH.

[SECOND EDITION.]

LONDON

FREETHOUGHT PUBLISHING COMPANY

63, FLEET STREET, E.C.

1887.

—

PRICE SIXPENCE

PREFATORY NOTE TO SECOND EDITION.

In 1877 the first edition of this pamphlet was issued, and it has now been out of print for a considerable period. The increased interest recently taken in the subject of financial economy seems to warrant the issue of this new, completely revised, and largely augmented edition. The Parliamentary Papers utilised here, and which may all be obtained from Hansard and Sons through any newsagent, are: "Accounts relating to Public Income and Expenditure, 1869," vols. i. and ii.; Finance Accounts for 1886-7 to 31st March, 1887; Estimates and Appropriation Accounts, Army, Navy, and Civil Service; Statistical Abstracts.

TAXATION:

HOW IT ORIGINATED, AND WHO BEARS IT.

In ancient times, in this country, the ordinary expenditure of the sovereign, as representing or wielding the executive power, was made up of Crown rents, feudal dues of various natures (set out in Madox's "History of the Exchequer", p. 202), prisage—a right the king claimed of taking to his own use and at his own valuation as much as the king had occasion for—of all merchandise belonging to merchant strangers, and sometimes merchandise of native-born merchants, out of every ship importing the same; and butlerage, a similar exaction applied to wine. These prisage and butlerage exactions were at first a mere sort of uncertain extortion by force, and were taken by some feudal lords, as well as by the Crown; but in time they became a prescribed or customary levy, payable by native merchants and by merchant strangers in different proportions; and the exactions having been at first taken in kind, were at last commuted into a money payment, and were called "tonnage and poundage", being so much per ton on wine, and so much per pound on other goods. The word "customs" in ancient time seems to have covered many customary payments and dues, regal, feudal, and ecclesiastical, but became gradually restricted until it was at last limited only to the duties payable to the king upon the importation, exportation, or carriage coastwise of various articles. In the reign of Richard I. an important duty on wine, called "prise", was payable to the king and was accounted for to the Exchequer. In the reign of John impost duties are mentioned on wood, salt, and fish, and export duties on wool and leather. The first Parliamentary authority we can find for the exaction of a customs duty is in 1297, when the community of the realm granted to Edward I., in aid of his war with France, a customs duty of 40 shillings for every sack of wool, and 5 marks for every last of leather, exported, for the space of two or three years, if the war should last so long. There must have been earlier Parliamentary grants than this, but I cannot trace them. When the grant of 1297 was made, the king declared that he would take no fresh custom of the nation without its common consent, but that he reserved the right to continue to collect the "old customs duties", said to have been granted before that time, of half a mark for every sack of wool, and a mark for every last of leather. The duties of "tonnage and poundage" were generally granted to the king by one and the same Act of Parliament, and were called the subsidy of tonnage and poundage. Some of the kings claimed the right to levy tonnage and poundage at their own will and discretion, and by their own authority; but this was, from the sixteenth century forward, almost always contested by Parliament. It was in 1629 that what Carlyle calls "a brave and noble Parliament" held the Speaker in the chair until remonstrances had been voted against the king's claim to collect tonnage and poundage by his own writ. It was this same Parliament which declared: "That no man hereafter be compelled to make or yield any gift, loan, benevolence, tax, or such-like charge, without common consent by Act of Parliament." Prior to this declaration, forced loans and compulsory benevolences were extremely common, and the Jews were especial and unpitied sufferers. As, for example: "Anno 1210, by the King's (John) command, all the Jews of both sexes were seized, imprisoned, and tortured; whereupon they gave the king all they had. One of them, refusing to comply, was ordered to have a tooth beaten out every day till he paid 10,000 marks. Seven of his teeth were accordingly struck out in seven days, and at length, the eighth day, to save the rest, he paid the sum at first demanded. So says Mat. Paris" ("Royal Treasury", p. 45).

In the early times the customs were let or farmed by the Crown to collectors for a cash purchase-payment, or as a recompense for services rendered, or as a reward to a favorite, or to secure, and as a repayment of, a loan, previously made or then agreed to be made, to the king. In 1329 the entire customs of England were farmed for £20 a day, Sundays excepted, the total amounting to £6,260 a year. In the year 1400 the customs were let for £8,000 a year. In the year 1650 they averaged £500,000 per annum; in 1800 they were £8,144,380; in 1876 they amounted to £20,341,502, or, with the excise, to £48,641,321 per year. For the year ending 31st March, 1887, the receipts from customs were £20,155,000, and from excise £25,550,000.

The practice of farming customs ceased in 1671, when the collection was transferred to a board of commissioners. For extraordinary war expenditure, the old military tenures involved special charges on the landowners, but these feudal obligations slowly disappeared, and subsidies and aids by Parliament were gradually substituted for them. In 1635, in consequence of the reluctance of Parliament to vote any subsidy until certain grievances had been redressed, an effort was made by King Charles I., while no Parliament was sitting, to levy a tax called ship-money by his own writ, without any concurrence or sanction of Parliament, and the courts of law affirmed the king's right to make this levy; but in November, 1640, the Long Parliament declared ship-money illegal, and enacted that no tax could be levied on exports or imports save by the common consent of Parliament. Amongst ancient direct taxes was one of hearth-money, which does not, however, appear under this name as a statutory tax until 1662, when Parliament granted two shillings per year to Charles II. for every firehearth or stove. This hearth-money was voted as a compensation for the suppression of the Court of Wards, and of other feudal tenures. Hearth-money was finally abolished in 1689 on the resolution of the House of Commons "that the said revenue cannot be so regulated, but that it will occasion many difficulties and questions, and that it is in itself not only a great oppression to the poorer sort, but a badge of slavery upon the whole people, exposing every man's house to be entered into and searched at pleasure by persons unknown to him".

Several poll-taxes were from time to time enacted; the

first we can find is in 1377 of 4d. per head for every man and woman above sixteen. The aristocrary paid higher rates, a ducal head being rated at £6 13s. 4d. The Wat Tyler rebellion grew out of resistance to a poll-tax. The last poll was enacted in 1698, but some collection of arrears was continued for a few years later. There have been several very absurd direct taxes. In 1723 there was a Papist tax, and in 1695 taxes were levied on weddings, burials, bachelors, and widows. In 1710 and 1718 two shillings a ton duty was laid on coals in order to build some new churches, and afterwards to provide for the clergymen.

Whenever extraordinary funds were necessary for the purpose of carrying on a war, or for any other special object, the king at first took by force and of his own will until Edward I., when "the Lords, without the Commons, assessed for the king"; and at last Parliament made an extraordinary grant as an aid or subsidy. Aids were very ancient, and were originally payable out of baronies and military fees by a free vassal to his lord on specified occasions—as to make his eldest son a knight, to marry his eldest daughter, and to ransom his person if taken in war. At last aid was a sort of indefinite word, subsidy being more modern. These Parliamentary subsidies were a specified proportion—as a tenth or fifteenth—of the nominal income; or a special duty for a limited period upon wines or goods. The most usual aid to the king was the grant of a fifteenth, and was at first rather a substitution for the feudal revenue payable by the landowner to the king. By the 14th Edward III., statute 1, cap. 20, A.D. 1340, a ninth and a fifteenth were granted for the wars in Scotland, France, and Gascony. The ninth lamb, ninth fleece, and ninth sheep were to be taken for two years, and the ninth part of all goods and chattels in cities and boroughs. Foreign merchants not dwelling in cities and boroughs, and other people dwelling in forests and wastes, were to pay one-fifteenth. Poor cottiers, and those living by bodily travail, were exempt.

The last grant of a tenth and a fifteenth appears to have been made in the reign of James I., and the last subsidy was in the reign of Charles II. The land-tax grew out of these subsidies, the king complaining that the aristocracy defrauded him by under-rating their incomes.

A land-tax should in every country be the chief source of internal revenue. In India land pays to-day a very large proportion; in 1866 it was nearly one-half of the total taxation, being £20,473,897 out of a gross revenue of £48,935,220. In 1885 it was £21,832,211 out of a gross revenue of £70,371,289. In France, before the late war, land paid one-sixth of all the taxation. In England, on the accession of George I., it paid two-fifths of the total taxation; to-day land bears less than one-seventy-eighth part of the national burdens.

Land to-day is assessed at the rate of 4s. in the £ on a valuation made in 1692. Under this assessment land paid, in 1798, £2,037,627 net, and the gross annual value of land was then stated at £22,500,000. In 1887 the land-tax realised, gross, £1,082,777, and the Parliamentary return under Schedule A gives the gross annual value of land, not including mines and quarries, for 1885 at £194,375,167. At the rate of 4s. in the £—thought fair by the landowners themselves eighty years ago—the land-tax alone ought to amount to nearly £39,000,000, or about one-half the present total of our onerous taxation. Land-owners may doubtless urge that they ought in any such calculation to have credit for the £5,510,804 levied as Income Tax on lands, tenements, etc., under Schedule A, and the £414,359 occupation of lands, tenements, etc., levied under Schedule B.

This unfairness in the levy of the land-tax will scarcely be wondered at when it is known to what an enormous extent land is owned by persons who are either members of the House of Lords or of the House of Commons, and when it is considered how few persons own a large pro-portion of the whole area of the United Kingdom. The total area of the United Kingdom is 77,635,182 acres, and of this 38,875,522 acres are owned by 2,184 indi-viduals, of whom 421 persons own no less than 22,880,775 acres. Can it be wondered at that land-laws are unfair when it is remembered that nearly every one of these landholders speaks or votes in one or other of the legis-lative assemblies either by himself or by his nominee. The land valuation of 1692 was certainly imperfect, and some have urged that it was purposely and fraudu-lently understated. This valuation was adopted without challenge by William Pitt in 1798; he had, however, the grace to say that his measure for the nominal land-tax of 4s. in the £ was not intended to prevent a future Parliament from augmenting the tax. So far from augmenting the amount, we have the fact that the land-tax to-day represents throughout Great Britain a most unequal and ridiculously low figure. The accountants of the Liverpool Financial Reform Association have made a careful analysis of the land-tax as it is paid, and the land-tax as it ought to be paid, and it appears from this calculation that— entirely omitting the value of mines, quarries, iron works, and other real properties transferred to Schedule D in 1866 —the highest land-tax paid is in Suffolk, 5½d. in the £ ; in many counties the tax is less than 1d. in the £, and in some less than one farthing in the £. In Lancashire the land-tax is half-a-farthing in the £, and in Scotland three-sixteenths of a 1d. The general average of the land-tax throughout the United Kingdom is 1d. and five-eights of a 1d. per £.

The contention in this essay will be that the landholding class, being practically the legislating class, with a monopoly of one House, and, until 1832, with absolute control of the House of Commons, have gradually shifted from off the land the fiscal burdens which land ought not only to bear, but which would be less oppressive if levied on land than they are when borne by labor.

While the tax-levying Parliaments were composed, as in the first half—and even in the latter part—of the seventeenth century, of the persons who actually paid the taxes, the votes were small and hard to carry through the House of Commons. Now the votes are large, and pass much too easily. Joseph Hume is dead, and no one bears his mantle.

It ought, however, to be remembered that Members of the House of Commons are not sufficiently encouraged and supported by their constituents on questions of financial reform. Members are denounced for obstruction if they speak frequently or at any length ; are derided for "cheeseparing" and "nibbling at the estimates"; and yet it is only by close investigation of each separate item, and by attempted restriction of each disbursement, that any permanent economy can be hoped for. Voters should carefully watch the conduct of their local members when the estimates are being discussed, and should, when necessary, hold meetings, and send up resolutions and petitions to give weight to the voice of the man who represents them in Parliament.

The total ordinary expenditure for 1887 was £89,996,752, for 1877 it amounted to £80,099,051 ; in 1848 it was £59,323,465; in 1837 it was £49,878,124; in 1706 it was £5,691,000. It is submitted that the increase during the present reign, and especially during the last twenty years, has been unduly extravagant, and it is urged that, unless the increase be stopped, and a marked reduction be effected, revolution must result from this enormous increase of the people's burdens.

The increase in our home expenditure during the present reign has been nominally about £40,000,000, but has been really almost £42,000,000, allowing for the lesser charge in 1887 for the interest and management of the National Debt.

It must be borne in mind that our local taxation shows an enormous increase. In 1868, for England and Wales alone, the total expenditure was £30,454,523. In 1883–4 the total expenditure of local authorities for England and Wales alone was £52,958,353. The total local expenditure of the United Kingdom for 1867–8 was £36,132,834; for 1883–4 it was £64,087,481.

The first item in our National Expenditure consists of the charge for interest and management of our National Debt, amounting to £27,958,022.

I agree with Mr. Dudley-Baxter that a national debt is a national evil. It is a mortgage of the earnings of generations unborn—a mortgage created by the Parliament of the nation—a mortgage on earnings in which Parliament has no property. Parliament, and the Government maintained by its authority, have not even the right of ownership of the actual earnings of the living citizens, much less has either Parliament or Government any right of ownership in labor not yet existing. It has only a protectorate and limited jurisdiction over the vast aggregate of existing property, and over the living workers, whose economies constitute the capital—and the ability to create fication for the creation of national debt, save "in case of great emergency, with which the State is otherwise unable to cope", and then only if it may be fairly maintained that those who are to be called upon to bear the burden shifted from the borrowing generation will enjoy benefits which would be impossible, save for the borrowing. The creation of a national debt is only justifiable when the money is expended on public works which increase the productive ability of the nation, or so facilitate commerce as to render actual produce more available. Mr. Baxter says : "Owners of property that was not in existence at the time of the loan, and workers who have inherited no property at all from their borrowing ancestors, are obliged by this law of public credit to pay interest as to the amount of which they have had no discretion, and to deprive themselves of comforts, and even necessaries, for the cost of services in which they have no share, and probably have derived no benefit. Such a power as this transfers a burden from one set of workers and property to a materially different set of workers and property, and inflicts a great deal of hardship, and often of injustice, upon future generations—more particularly on the poor among them. Hence the power of borrowing ought only to be exercised on the clearest necessity, and with the utmost economy". And, further : "The unnecessary or extra portion of war expenditure, occasioned by the adoption of borrowing, is capital unnecessarily diverted from productive investments, and spent on unproductive objects. Instead of being employed in trade or industrial undertakings, or improvements, adding a new annual produce to the net income of the nation, this capital becomes a pensioner on the net income of the country. It is like taking an army of artificers and agricultural laborers from their workshops and fields, to maintain them, and their children after them, without labor, upon the taxes. An unproductive debt, by its absorption of useful capital, prevents improvements, hinders the growth of industrial capital, and stunts the development of a nation; while, at the same time, to meet the necessity of paying interest, it imposes additional taxation, and lessens the margin of tax-bearing power of the nation." The whole of the debt owing to-day by Great Britain is the unpaid balance of money borrowed for war expenditure. To-day we owe about £738,000,000;[1] we have spent for wars alone, between 1688 and 1868, £1,555,421,160, and this without reckoning the cost of borrowing, and without calculating the interest paid on the money borrowed.

The total military and naval expenditure during the war in Ireland and against France, 1688 to 1697, amounted to £36,876,203.

During the war from 1702 to 1713, called "the war of the Spanish succession", the total cost for army, navy, and ordnance was £66,279,292. It was at this time that the increase of our standing army commenced, and the system of subsidising foreign powers and hiring foreign troops originated.

The naval and military expenditure during the war with Spain, from 1718 to 1721, came to £11,399,324.

Between 1739 and 1748 we had the "war with Spain (right of search) and Austrian succession", and in those years spent for fighting £62,077,642. When the treaty of peace was made at Aix-la-Chapelle, the right of search was not even referred to.

The "seven years' war" was nominally 1756 to 1763, but really involved military expenditure over eleven years, at a cost of £104,611,374.

The war which severed the connexion between the North American colonies and the British monarchy — the war which served to create the Republic of the United States of America — was accompanied by a total outlay of £139,521,035.

The war with France—nominally commencing in 1793, but really commencing with the signature of the secret arrangement in 1791 (concurred in by George III. and the Tory Government), by which the various Continental Powers, parties to the secret treaty of Mantua, agreed to invade France, in order to overthrow the Constitution— made up the enormous total for naval and military expenditure of £989,636,449, when the expenditure ended in 1817. So that if we had not joined in the conspiracy to enable Louis XVI. to break his oath, we should now have

---

[1] While the National Debt has been reduced from £785,923,831 in 1872 to the above amount, a reduction of nearly £48,000,000, the aggregate of local indebtedness has increased during the period 1874-5 to 1884-5 from £92,820,100 to £173,207,968, an augmentation of £80,387,868.

no debt, and France might possibly have escaped the Reign of Terror.

The Crimean war cost £116,053,151, for the maintenance of the Turk at Constantinople and the prevention of Russian war vessels in the Black Sea. The first result has enabled the Sublime Porte to borrow English money, and to misgovern and maltreat Bulgarian, Bosnian, and Herzegovinian peasants. The Russian diplomatists have since persuaded the English Government to abandon the second result, despite the blood and treasure lavished to secure it.

Some contend that it is unjust to include, as I have done, the whole expenditure for army, navy, and ordnance during war years; but I submit that I should be justified in adding to the above items all increase of the annual charge of the public debt, all interest paid on money borrowed towards defraying the war expenditure, and also the difference between the amount actually received when borrowing as against the total indebtedness created. If this were done, the total cash wasted for and through war, during the last 200 years, would not be less than £2,000,000,000.

Mr. Goschen proposes to reduce the permanent charge to £26,000,000, thus making a nominal economy of £1,704,000 per year, by avoiding so much immediate payment of debt, and leaving a larger burden for our successors.

The second item is, " Other charges on the Consolidated Fund ", £1,743,891.

Of this the Civil List for her Majesty is £385,000, thus made up: "Her Majesty's Privy Purse, £60,000; Salaries of her Majesty's Household, £131,260; Expenses of her Majesty's Household, £172,500; Royal Bounty, Alms, and Special Services, £13,200; Unappropriated, £8,040."

This £385,000 is very far from representing the total annual cost of her Majesty, most of the remainder being distributed through the votes. There is, however, within these "other charges on the Consolidated Fund" an item of " £803, Receiver-General of the Duchy of

Lancaster, annuity in lieu of prisage and butlerage on wines imported into the ports of that county, per Act 2nd and 3rd Will. IV., cap. 84". All other items for the cost of her Majesty must be searched out by patient groping through the Civil Service Estimates and the estimates for the army and navy. These items come out somewhat as follows:

	£	s.	d.
Perpetual Pension charged on the Consolidated Fund in lieu of prisage and butlerage on wines imported into the county and Duchy of Lancaster	803	0	0
Net income of the Duchy paid over to her Majesty after all deductions, about ..	45,000	0	0

Two items which to-day are treated as private property of the monarch and of the Prince of Wales respectively are the several incomes of the Duchy of Lancaster and of the Duchy of Cornwall. In the reigns of William III. and of Queen Anne the incomes of each of these Duchies went to make up the total Civil List enjoyed by the monarch, and it was not until the accession of William IV. that the Duchy of Lancaster was claimed as private property. When Lord Holland was appointed Chancellor of the Duchy of Lancaster in 1830, it is clear that he regarded the Duchy as national property, and that this view was at first maintained by the Liberal Government of which Earl Grey was the head, although the Cabinet soon receded from their patriotic position. I find the king expressing in writing[1] his "considerable alarm and uneasiness" because it appeared to be in the contemplation of Lord Holland not only to admit of the threatened interference of Parliament in the concerns of the Duchy of Lancaster, but even to promote it. So far from concurring in any surrender, William IV. strenuously protests "that any successful attempt to deprive the Sovereign of his independent possession will be to lower and degrade him into the state and condition of absolute and entire dependence as a pensioner on the House of Commons", and he adds that he "cannot indeed conceive upon what plea such a national invasion of the private rights and a seizure of the private estate of the Sovereign could be justified".

---

[1] "Correspondence of Earl Grey with William IV.", p. 9.

Then, for the first time since the Revolution of 1688, was the Duchy of Lancaster claimed by the monarch " as his separate personal and private estate, vested in his Majesty by descent from Henry VII. in his body natural, and not in his body politic as king ".

In 1830 the then Chancellor of the Exchequer stated in the House of Commons that the revenues of the Duchies of Cornwall and of Lancaster were not included, " because those of Cornwall never became the property of the Crown unless when there was no heir-apparent of the throne; and the revenues of Lancaster had been from a very early period subject to peculiar regulations totally independent of its authority". On the accession of her present Majesty, Mr. D. Whittle Harvey, M.P., formally claimed the right of Parliament to inquire into and appropriate the revenues of the Duchy of Cornwall and of the Duchy of Lancaster; but he was opposed by the Government, and, on motion, defeated by 184 votes to 52.

Until August, 1883, her Majesty received also £100 10s. 10d. " creation fees " payable to the Duchy of Lancaster; but, in consequence of the outcry against Perpetual Pensions, this has been commuted at 26·945 years' purchase for £2,709 1s. 10d. The following appears in the evidence taken before the Committee on Perpetual Pensions:

"It is stated in Stubbs' 'Constitutional History' (vol. iii., p. 434) that a when a Duke was created he generally received a pension of £40 a year on his promotion, which was known as 'creation money'. In the case of a Marquis the creation money was £35 (Ibid., p. 435). The same author states (p. 436) that the Earl's creation money, £20, was a substitute for the third penny of the county, of which little is heard after the thirteenth century, and that the retention of this payment probably suggested the bestowal of creation money on those who were raised to newer ranks of the peerage. The creation money of a Viscount was 20 marks (Ibid., p. 526).

"The creation money formerly payable to the Duchy of Lancaster was made up of the following items, viz.:

		£	s.	d.	
County of Lincoln ..	..	20	0	0	a year.
,,	Nottingham ..	20	0	0	,,
,,	Derby ..	20	0	0	,,
,,	Hertford or Essex	40	10	10	,,
	Total ..	£100	10	10	

"No information is preserved in the Duchy of Lancaster Office of the origin of these grants."

	£	s.	d.
Repairs of palaces, kitchen gardens, etc., in the personal occupation of her Majesty— Civil Service Estimates, Class I... ..	13,032	0	0
(This amount varies every year, and in 1870 was as high as £30,535.)			
Repairs of palaces partly occupied by her Majesty, Class I.	2,434	0	0
(For the year ending 31st March, 1882, these cost £3,519.)			
Repairs of palaces occupied by persons under her Majesty's permission, often members of the Royal Family, Class I., at least ..	7,000	0	0
St. George's Chapel, Windsor	500	0	0
Royal yachts and naval charges, about ..	34,656	0	0
(The original cost of these royal yachts was £275,528.)			
Military aides-de-camp to her Majesty (in addition to half-pay)	1,150	0	0
(These have also allowances in lieu of servants and table-money.)			
Queen's Plates, to be run for in Scotland— Civil Service Estimates, Class II. ..	218	0	0
Queen's Plates, to be run for in Ireland ..	1,562	6	2
Her Majesty's charities and bounties in Scotland—Civil Service Estimates, Class VI...	1,300	0	0
Her Majesty's bounty (Ireland) (same vote)	90	0	0
Her Majesty's Limner	97	0	0
Her Majesty's Historiographer	184	0	0
Her Majesty's Clockmaker	16	13	4
Allowance to Turncock and Engineer, Windsor Castle—Civil Service Estimates, Class VI...	201	12	9
Attendants, Albert Memorial, Windsor Castle	120	0	0
Laborers, Turncock, and Ratcatcher at Buckingham Palace	201	0	0
In Navy Estimates, expenses on account of her Majesty and Royal Household ..	1,352	0	5
(This amount varies yearly. There are also, unspecified as to amount, "entertainment allowances to ward-room officers of H.M.S. 'Osborne'".)			

There is in the charges for 1884 a charge of £15,000, paid to the Queen as Duchess of Lancaster "for Crown rights to escheats, etc., within certain liberties of the Duchy".

England, in an article on the cost of the monarchy, in which article the net income from the Crown lands is deducted from such cost, says :

"It is the practice of Radical financiers to assert that the Crown lands were not the property of her Majesty. In answer to this it may be sufficient to quote the Act 1st and 2nd Vict., cap. 2, which distinctly recognises the fact that the hereditary rates, duties, payments, and revenues in England, Scotland, and Ireland *belong and are payable to her Majesty,* and states that she places the same at the disposal of Parliament, feeling confident that adequate provision will be made for the support of the honor and dignity of the Crown."

The "belong and are" in the words italicised in *England* were introduced for the first time in the preamble of the Act referred to, but, if they meant anything, would not alone refer to Crown lands, but would include excise and post-office and other revenues. If the editor of *England* relies on these recital words to prove the private property of the Queen in the Crown lands, they equally prove her property in more than £27,500,000 further, the amount of the other hereditary revenues still existing. The hereditary revenues are for the first time specified in the 9th and 10th William III., cap. 24, as follows :

"Hereditary excise.
"Hereditary Post-office duties.
"Small branches of the hereditary revenues, viz. :
    First-fruits and tenths of the clergy ;
    Fines for writs of covenant and writs of entry payable
      in the Alienation Office ;
    Post fines ;
    The revenue of wine licences ;
    The moneys arising by sheriff's process and compositions
      in the Exchequer ;
    Seizures of uncustomed and prohibited goods ;
    The revenues of the Duchy of Cornwall ;
    Any other revenue arising by the rent of lands in Eng-
      land and Wales, or for fines of leases, and the duty of
      $4\frac{1}{2}$ per cent. in specie arising in Barbadoes and the
      Leeward Islands in America."

And there were also

"Hanaper revenues ;
Fines and forfeitures in criminal matters ;
Droits of the Crown and of the Admiralty ;
Rents and quit rents in the colonies."

All these revenues (some of which no longer exist) were applied to the Civil List "during the reigns of Queen Anne, George I. and George II." (*vide* "Accounts relating to Public Income and Expenditure", 366 I., 1869, vol. ii., p. 457). The Civil List then "comprised the whole charge for the civil expenditure" of Great Britain and Ireland (p. 485). No one source of income more than any other was the private property of the monarch. No pretence of surrender of anything was ever alleged until the vague recital in preamble of the Civil List Act of George III. (1 George III., cap. 1). Since then the surrender fable has been repeated, and the recital words have been strengthened until persons like the editor of *England* actually believe them. The farce of the pretence of surrender is shown by the fact that all these revenues are, without distinction, since 1787, by statute carried to and made part of the Consolidated Fund.

As it is contended by leading statesmen, Liberal and Conservative, that the amounts voted from time to time to her Majesty and other Royal personages are so voted as some part of a bargain or honorable understanding by which, in consideration of certain lands or valuable properties surrendered by her Majesty, the nation accepted the responsibility of providing for the various princes and princesses, who otherwise would have no means of existence, it will perhaps be respectful to answer them more fully. Not only there is no such bargain or honorable understanding, but, as I shall presently show, it is utterly impossible any such bargain could have been made. If the bargain has been made by Parliament, it must have been embodied in some statute. No such statute exists. As to the surrender, I shall show that, despite the words introduced into the Civil List Act of the present reign, her Majesty has never surrendered property to the value of one single halfpenny, but that, on the contrary, she retains and keeps as private property, in addition to her Civil List allowance, revenues which, for at least four reigns since the Revolution of 1688, formed part of the Civil List income; meaning by Civil List income all expenditure except army, navy, and ordnance. Several members of the Royal Family have also very large private fortunes.

It is sometimes urged that any objection to the Royal Family expenditure comes to-day with a very bad grace,

as the amount of the Civil List expenditure is much less
than it has been in previous reigns. As a matter of fact,
the amount directly received or indirectly enjoyed by the
several members of the Royal Family is larger than it has
been in any previous reign, even in the extravagant period
of George III.

What, if any, was the bargain or understanding between
the sovereign and the nation? and what, if anything, was
surrendered by the sovereign as part of the bargain? To
answer this it is necessary to go back to the first Civil List
grant, and to the statute by which the Civil List was
established. This inquiry may start with the Revolution
of 1688, because the two previous Civil List votes to
Charles II. and James II. become utterly immaterial. It
cannot be pretended that William of Orange surrendered
anything on his accession to the Throne, nor does the Civil
List Act, 9th and 10th William III., cap. 23, recite or pretend any such surrender. William III., when he landed
in this country, was in no sense legally or morally the
heir to any private estate which was then held by or had
been held by James II., who was living himself, who had
issue living, and who it is not pretended ever ceded anything to William, nor did any statute give him any such
right. Instead of there being any surrender by William
III. to the nation, there is a specific grant to William for
life by Parliament as representing the nation. The grant
is first by vote on the 25th April, 1689, and then by statute
on the 21st December, 1697. There is in the Act no suggestion of any right of property which might have been
left by William to his heirs or successors. There is a
mere grant for life, determining with William's death.
On this death everything granted reverted to the nation,
just as leasehold property, on the termination of a lease
for life, reverts to the lessor. On the accession of Queen
Anne, 8th March, 1702, we have the second Civil List
Statute—1st Anne, Statute 1. In this there is again a
grant to the Queen for life, but not the faintest suggestion
that Anne had surrendered anything, or indeed that she
had anything to surrender. On the contrary, there is a
specific enactment forbidding and limiting the alienation
of any of the revenues granted. After a recital that "the
necessary expenses of supporting the Crown, or the greatest
part of them, were formerly defrayed by a land revenue,

which hath from time to time be diminished by the grants of former kings and queens of this realm ", it is enacted by the 1st Anne, Statute 1, cap. 7, secs. 5 and 7, that "no grant shall be made of land for more than thirty-one years, or for three lives, and at a reasonable rent "; and that no other grant shall be made for any estate or term longer than the life of the monarch, "and that any grant of either land or revenues contrary to such enactments shall be null and void". The third Civil List Act is 1st George I., cap. 1, 1st August, 1714; and this, too, is utterly silent as to any surrender. Nor, by the nature of the case, could there have been any surrender. George I., when he came to England, held property as elector of Hanover, but the whole of that property he most certainly kept. There is evidence that he repeatedly took from the English Treasury to increase his Hanoverian property, but there is not the slightest color of any contention that he ever surrendered to England the value of one farthing. The Hanoverian property, although actually much augmented by English moneys, is not now even remotely connected with this country. It passed away in the male line on the accession of her present Majesty to the English throne. The 1st George I., cap. 1, is, as in the two previous Civil List Statutes, a grant by Parliament on behalf of the nation, and it is only a grant for life. The fourth Civil List Act is dated 11th June, 1727, 1st George II., cap. 1, and here, once more, there is an utter absence of any sort of surrender or pretence of surrender; it is again a grant for life only. In 1760 we find a change in words, although the facts were exactly the same except that the person was new. In the preamble to the Civil List Act on the accession of George III. it is recited that the King had been graciously pleased to signify his consent that "such disposition might be made of his interest in the hereditary revenues as might best conduce to the utility and satisfaction of the public". This recital was so much pure inventive audacity. George III. had no legal interest whatever, and the words were of no value. George III. could not have inherited from his grandfather, George II., that which his grandfather only held for life, and of which the reversion was not in George III., but in the nation. The previous grant was not to George II., his heirs and successors; it was a grant to

George II., for life only.   The wording of the new recital
in the Civil List Act of George III. was vague, but it has
served its purpose, and has been textually repeated in the
three succeeding Civil List Statutes.   It is the sole founda-
tion for the whole of the repeated declarations of a surrender which is purely imaginary, and has no real founda-
tion in fact.   It is perfectly true that the myth has been
enlarged and beautified in the subsequent Civil List Acts
of George IV., William IV., and, as pointed out on p. 16,
of her present Majesty, but even at the last the so-called
surrender is pure fable.

Having now disposed of the surrender myth, I come to
the bargain or honorable-understanding legend.   When
was the bargain made?   Between whom, and where is it
recorded?   In 1736 George II. knew of no bargain on the
part of Parliament, even to the extent of providing for the
Prince of Wales.   On the 22nd February, 1737, it was
proposed to make an annual allowance to Frederick, Prince
of Wales, and George II. objected, on the ground that
the responsibility to provide for the Prince of Wales rested
with himself, and that "it would be highly indecorous to
interfere between father and son".   The bargain is, like
the surrender, a myth, though it has now grown, by dint
of repetition, into a firm article of faith on the part of the
occupants of both front benches of the House of Commons.
But if there is no actual bargain, it may still be urged,
is there not some honorable understanding?   I reply that
arrangements with reigning families cannot be, and ought
not to be, the subject of any understanding.   They should
be dealt with by specific enactment.

That no such honorable understanding or bargain was
known or suspected by her Majesty's predecessor, William
IV., is quite clear; for we find William IV. applying by
letter, first to the Duke of Wellington, and, on the latter's
resignation, to Earl Grey, asking that a sum of money
might be issued to the Queen for an outfit.   To this Earl
Grey replies that he will "have considerable difficulties to
encounter from the jealousy of the House of Commons".
Now would have been the time for William to plead the
bargain or honorable understanding, if any such existed;
but, instead of this, the King writes that he is "perfectly
satisfied with Earl Grey's letter, and quite sensible of the
difficulty which may occur".   Even the Tory Duke of

Wellington had only promised the King that he would "endeavor, if possible, to obtain some money to aid at least in defraying the cost of the Queen's outfit". And at last, one of Earl Grey's Cabinet having positively objected, the proposed application was abandoned by the King, in order, as his Majesty says, to avoid "unpleasant discussion" in the House of Commons.

The Finance Accounts give £158,000 as the amount of annuities to members of the Royal Family, viz. :

Her Royal Highness the Princess Royal, Crown Princess of Prussia	£8,000	0	0
(A grant of £40,000 was made to her Royal Highness on her marriage)			
His Royal Highness Albert Edward, Prince of Wales	40,000	0	0
(A grant of £23,455 was made on his coming of age and marriage)			
Her Royal Highness the Princess of Wales ..	10,000	0	0
His Royal Highness Alfred Ernest Albert, Duke of Edinburgh	25,000	0	0
(The Navy Estimates contain items not included in this sum)			
Her Royal Highness Helena Augusta Victoria Princess Christian of Schleswig-Holstein-Sunderbourg-Augustenburg..	6,000	0	0
(A grant of £30,000 was made to her Royal Highness on her marriage)			
Her Royal Highness Louise Caroline Alberta, Princess, Marchioness of Lorne	6,000	0	0
(A grant of £30,000 was made to her Royal Highness on her marriage)			
His Royal Highness Arthur William Patrick Albert, Duke of Connaught and Strathearn	25,000	0	0
Her Royal Highness the Duchess of Albany ..	6,000	0	0
Her Royal Highness Beatrice Mary Feodore (Princess Henry of Battenburg)	6,000	0	0
(A grant of £30,000 was made to her Royal Highness on her marriage)			
Her Royal Highness the Duchess of Cambridge	6,000	0	0
Her Royal Highness the Princess Augusta, Duchess of Mecklenburg-Strelitz	3,000	0	0
His Royal Highness the Duke of Cambridge	12,000	0	0

(This, of course, does not include the military

salaries of his Royal Highness, which are,
as Field-Marshal Commanding-in-Chief,
£4,500, and as Colonel of the Grenadier
Guards £2,200.   Nor does it include the
game-preserving and other benefits enjoyed
by his Royal Highness as Ranger of Richmond Park, who for his pleasure excludes
the public from access to a large portion of
the park, enclosed for game.   The game-
keepers are paid for by the public.)

He^r Royal Highness the Princess Mary,
Princess of Teck £5,000 0 0

This year there is the following charge in the Supple-
mentary Estimates.   Special packets for the conveyance of
Distinguished Persons as under:

Quarter to 31st March 1886—
    Prince of Wales, Folkestone to Boulogne   ..   £40
    Prince of Wales, Boulogne to Folkestone   ..   40
Quarter to 30th June, 1886—
    Crown Princess of Germany, Calais to Dover..   40
    Duchess of Edinburgh, Dover to Calais   ..   40
Quarter to 31st December 1886—
    Prince and Princess of Wales, Dover to Calais..   40
    Grand Duchess of Mecklenberg, Calais to Dover   40
    Prince of Wales, Calais to Dover   40
    Duke and Duchess of Connaught, Dover to
      Calais   40
Quarter to 31st March, 1887—
    Prince of Wales, Dover to Calais   40
    Prince of Wales, Calais to Dover   40
    Prince of Wales, Dover to Calais   40
    Prince of Wales, Calais to Dover   40
                              ——
                         £480."

"Receiver-General of the Duchy of Cornwall, compensation
for loss of duties on the coinage of tin per Acts 1st and 2nd
Victoria, cap. 120, £16,216 15s."   (Finance Accounts 1886-7,
p. 81.)

In a Parliamentary Return, No. 366, 1869, Part II.,
p. 473, there is the further explanation:

"Until the year 1838 all tin produced in Cornwall was required
to be coined, and certain duties were payable in respect thereof
as part of the revenue to the Duchy of Cornwall.   These coinage
duties were abolished by the Act 1st and 2nd Victoria, cap. 120,
and, in lieu thereof, an amount equal to the average net amount

of the preceding ten years was directed to be paid out of the Consolidated Fund to her Majesty, or other the personage for the time being entitled tothe revenues to the Duchy of Cornwall. This amount was fixed at £16,216 15s. per annum."

The perpetual payment to the Prince of Wales of £16,216 15s. 1½d. was fixed in 1838, and the following questions to Sir R. Welby on his examination before the Select Committee on Perpetual Pensions throw some light on the matter:

"Can you tell me what net income (the net only) of the Duchy of Cornwall is shown on that year; shall I be right in stating that the net income was £11,536?—It looks very much like that here; I have not worked it out. I make out the expenditure to be about £13,000.

"Does the Return you have before you enable you to say that in that sum of £11,536 there were not only included the receipts from tin coinage, post groats and white rents, whatever they were, but also rents of lands, fines on renewal of leases, royalties on minerals, and interest on investments?— Yes, all those headings appear here.

"So that the payment in perpetuity of £16,216 15s. 1½d. was in lieu of some portion only of £11,536?—It formed part of a gross revenue of which the honorable member is now stating the net.

"Is a sum of £630 14s. 2d. a part of the sum now paid of £16,216 15s. 1½d.?—It is.

"Was that sum precisely fixed in lieu of post groats for Cornwall?—That is the case.

"Is it true that the Duchy of Cornwall, during the ten years preceding the 1st of October 1838, received £10 per year and no more in respect of such post groats?—The post groats duty in Cornwall was granted by lease dated 31st July, 1813, to Mr. Benjamin Tucker, to hold for a term of seventeen years from the 5th July, 1823, at the reserved rent of £10 per annum, expiring on the 5th April, 1841.

"Then, is that practically yes to my question?—Yes.

"Did not the Treasury, in pursuance of that 2nd Section of 1st and 2nd Vict. c. 120 report that the post groats duties had only brought in £10 a year annually to the Duchy for ten years?—Yes, that was the case.

"And is not the £630 14s. 2d., whether rightfully or wrongfully paid, paid in respect of that which for ten years previously had only realised £10 a year?—Under a lease which was just about to expire.

"Is that so?—That is so.

"Did his late Majesty King William IV. signify his pleasure

that such post groats should cease on and from the 5th April, 1841 ?—That would be the view of the Treasury.

"Then was her present Majesty pleased to confirm such intention soon after her accession?—In the passage from the minute which I have read that is stated also.

"Did the Lords of the Treasury, by the minute which you have just read, direct that the sum of £16,216 15s. 11½d. should be diminished by the sum of £630 14s. 2d. from the 5th of April, 1841 ?—They stated that, 'inasmuch as the receipt of post groats in Cornwall, £630 14s. 2d., will cease on the 5th of April, 1841, on the termination of the existing interest, this annual sum will be diminished by such amount from that date '."

It turns out that the full sum has always been paid, and the Secretary of the Treasury admitted that this was done without any fresh minute.

"As far as you are concerned, there is an absolute gap of any authority after some month in 1841 ?—Yes."

Our Military Expenditure.

The third item is for our army and navy, £31,694,673, and of this the army cost us altogether £18,429,271, being more than double what it cost us in 1852, while the navy cost us £13,265,401, an increase since 1877, when it was £11,364,383, as against £5,849,916 in 1852. The German army and navy on a peace footing cost about £21,000,000. The increase in the peace cost of our army has been very terrible. In 1871 the cost was £13,430,400. In 1847 our army, militia, commissariat, and ordnance cost £9,061,233, everything included; showing the outrageous addition in twenty years of £7,775,000 per annum to the one item of military expenditure. Compare this with the cost of the army in 1792, just prior to the great continental wars, and the total then for Great Britain and Ireland was £2,410,212, or about one-seventh of the army expenditure for 1877.

Estimates are so wonderfully framed that it is possible many inaccuracies may be found in these figures; official witnesses who prepare the estimates admit that it is difficult for the ordinary member to understand them. Mr. Knox, Accountant-General, examined before the Select Committee on Army and Navy Estimates, admitted

(56) that an ordinary Member of Parliament looking at the estimates would be misled, and (57) that under Vote 1 "142,194 men in 1885-6 cost £5,023,674, and in 1886-7 151,867 cost £4,457,300". That is, "that 10,000 men less cost nearly half a million more". The extra staff in Egypt adds £19,000 a year to the cost of officers on the general staff, and we have to pay £2,000 a year cost of the officer in command at Malta, in consequence of the people of Malta refusing to pay. In answer to Mr. H. H. Fowler, while the total cost of the army is estimated for 1887-8 at £18,465,000, the real total cost should have been stated at £19,026,000 (309). We have 16,000 more soldiers than in 1874-5, at a cost of one million more money. It is very hard to say what our officers cost. In Vote 1 eight lieutenant-generals are stated to have cost £14,427, but (341) this did not include "their allowances which they may receive in kind, and sometimes they may receive in money". Asked, "Would it have been possible for any private individual to have ascertained from the estimates laid before Parliament from 1870 to the present year, that the total increase of the net army expenditure amounted to almost £9,000,000", Mr. Knox, the Accountant-General, frankly answered (477): "I think it would have been extremely difficult; I mean that no one could have brought out an exact comparison by merely taking the figures that were presented to Parliament for that year, and comparing them with the next year"; and again asked (483), "Would it be possible for any private Member of Parliament to ascertain from the estimates laid before Parliament that there had been an increase of the net ordinary expenditure upon the army of £5,100,000?" he answered, "I do not think it would".

The fourth item is "Miscellaneous Civil Service",
£17,826,453.

On this, speaking at Wolverhampton on June 3rd, Lord Randolph Churchill said: "I think there is room for great vigilance and considerable reform, and no inconsiderable reduction in the expenditure of public money connected with the civil service of this country. But I see in that expenditure, after having studied it pretty closely, no great or glaring or profligate extravagance," such as the noble lord pointed to in the army and navy. I venture to affirm that some at least of the civil service votes do show "great and glaring and profligate expenditure". His lordship went on to say: "I recognise that the democracy of Britain is continually making fresh demands on the State, that the democracy expects the State to perform duties which in former days the State was allowed to leave to private enterprise, and I recognise that the tendency of modern social reform must tend to check any hopes of large decrease in your civil expenditure". Against this half bribe offered to the democracy I desire to enter my strongest protest. The most dangerous tendency of the age, and the one which all true statesmen should strive to check, is that of the European democracy to look to the executive for service which the people should, and can, better perform for themselves. Self-reliant private enterprise should be encouraged; the State should not be regarded as a crutch for the incompetent, the incapable, and the unwilling. Democrats should know that the State has no resources save those obtained from the earnings and economies of the people, and that State help is often more costly to those who do not share the advantage than to those whom the State assists. To administer State aid additional officials are required, and all these have to be sustained by the labor of the masses.

Public Works and Buildings.

In the expenditure, under the head of "Public Works and Buildings", there are some items to which special attention should be drawn. 1st. Palaces in the personal occupation of Her Majesty, which cost £12,936 last year, and for which £12,589 are asked for 1888. £2,071 is charged in addition for palaces partly in the occupation of her Majesty. 2nd. Palaces not in the occupation of her Majesty, but which include St. James' Palace (Residence of H. R. H. the Duchess of Cambridge), Clarence House, and other residences of members of the Royal Family and their Households, cost £21,322, and it is difficult to say what other cost these involve under other votes. 3rd. The repairs to Marlborough House, the residence of the Prince of Wales, for 1878, cost £6,450; the actual charge for this year under this head is £2,020. In 1886 the expenditure on repairs of Marlborough House was £6,286 5s. 1d. As an illustration of the difficulty of knowing how much the Royal Family cost, it may be mentioned that last year £2,142 7s. 9d. on account of the visit of the Prince of Wales to Ireland in 1885 was charged against the vote for public buildings, Ireland, where few would have thought of searching for such an item. 4th. There are items amounting to £41,677, in 1887, for diplomatic and consular buildings, which shall be dealt with later, together with the other items for foreign office services. It is, however, necessary to note that this does not include the enormous annual cost for furniture. As harbor works are often suggested with a view of affording some employment for the unemployed, it is worth remark that in the estimates for 1885-86, it was estimated that the total cost of the harbor at Peterhead would be £500,000 spread over twenty-three years, but in the vote for the service last year the total estimate was stated at £745,920; Sir Gerald Fitzgerald and the other responsible officials were unable to explain the discrepancy between the two estimates? The construction of a new harbor at Dover was authorised by Treasury Minute of the 17th July, 1883, the works to be constructed by convict labor at a then estimated cost of £1,040,000, and to occupy in execution a probable period of sixteen years. Diplomatic and Consular Buildings cost in 1886 £30,224, and in the year 1887 £41,677.

Expenses of Public Departments.

The House of Lords nominally cost, in 1887, for salaries and similar expenses, £43,978, but this does not include £6,000 further charged on the Consolidated Fund for the Lord Chancellor, making a total of £49,978. The House of Commons, including a sum of £5,000, also charged on the Consolidated Fund for the Speaker, costs £57,493. The Treasury cost for 1888 is estimated at £59,045, on which it is well to notice that there is in addition £10,779 for superannuation charges, which non-effective charges form a constantly and dangerously increasing item on every vote. In addition they share, though only for £638 13s. 4d. in the expenditure of £19,060 on furniture for public departments, and £2,558 for stationery. The total cost of stationery and printing is £556,260. The Home Office costs £94,404, besides £6,087 for superannuation, and £2,388 for stationery, an apparent but not real decrease being shown by the transfer of the Inspectorship of Fisheries to the Board of Trade. The Foreign Office this year is to cost £73,061; £10,946 for superannuation, and £11,744 for stationery. The Colonial office, £41,524, besides £12,464 last year for superannuation, and £1,604 for stationery. The Privy Council cost £46,816; £837 for superannuation, and £2,719 for stationery. The Board of Trade £108,107; for superannuation, £18,070; for stationery, £9,769. The Charity Commission, £36,525; superannuation, £1,309; stationery, £1,637. Civil Service Commission, £40,531; superannuation, £350; stationery, £2,753. Exchequer and Audit Department, £53,934; superannuation, £15,108; stationery, £514. Friendly Societies Registry, £8,227; stationery, £305. Land Commissioners for England, £34,797; superannuation, £1,913; stationery, £501. Local Government Board, £444,241; superannuation, £12,582; stationery, £4,767. The salary of the Secretary for Scotland is £2,000 a year, and his private secretary receives £835 a year, £525 of this being his military pay.

A few of the petty continental legations have been swept away during the last twenty-five years, and there are several more which ought also to be abolished. The Chargé d'Affaires at Coburg, and his brethren in Wurtemburg, Darmstadt, and Dresden, might well be spared, our consuls being most certainly sufficient for all useful purposes.

The eccentricities of disbursements in the Foreign Office department are very wonderful. Vice-consuls in small places are found receiving more pay than vice-consuls in larger towns. Consuls in important ports receive often lesser salaries than consuls in ports of little or no consequence. Sometimes consuls receive less than vice-consuls. No sort of reasonable explanation can be given for such anomalies.

Some interesting information is derivable from the report of the Committee on Public Accounts. The Committee "called attention to a sum of £123 4s. 3d., paid to the holder of the offices of Assistant Clerk and Private Secretary to the Lord Privy Seal, as salary during a period from 18th June to 15th November, 1884, when he was in prison on a charge of forgery, to which he ultimately pleaded guilty, and they recommended its disallowance from the account". "The Comptroller and Auditor General calls attention to an amount in the accounts of the Northern Lights Commissioners of £179 for a dinner to forty-seven persons. The charge for the dinner in question is certainly extravagant." "It appears, by the evidence, that forty-seven dinners cost £70 10s., and there were ninety-six bottles of wine consumed at the same dinner, besides brandy and whiskey, by forty-seven people." The same official "calls attention to a payment of £232,926 to the Egyptian Government, for expenses connected with the Gordon Relief Expedition in 1884 and 1885, not supported by vouchers". He also "calls attention to the circumstances under which Viscount Wolseley and his staff drew their full pay and allowances for two months after their return from Egypt". "A sum of £176 17s. 9d., the expense incurred in a visit of the Canadian voyageurs to the pyramids, under the sanction of Lord Wolseley, is reported by the Comptroller and Auditor General as irregular."

Mr. Arthur O'Connor, M.P., whose services are very valuable on the Committee of Public Accounts, ascertained that Mr. Michel, whose pay is charged for in the estimates for the Patent Office for 1885-6, for 1886-7, and for the present year, at £800 a-year, as a matter of fact, died a considerable time ago.

At Berlin, in 1866, £50 was charged for a washstand and fittings supplied to our ambassador. The Public Accounts Committee examined Mr. Hamilton on this:

"What check does the Treasury exercise over such expenditure as this abroad; does it sanction any expenditure that is submitted and recommended by the ambassador?—The Treasury considers every application on its own merits.

"What were the merits of this particular washstand?—I am afraid I cannot say off-hand; I am not acquainted with them. . . . . I have a vague recollection of an item of this kind in an account, as to which our surveyor said that he thought the washstand ought not to have been put there at all."

Under Sub-head C., Foreign Office, Messengers' Travelling Expenses:

"It had been found that the charges for cabs are in many

instances far in excess of the rates allowed by the cab regulations and that as regards railway journeys also the sums paid appear to have been very large, and the Comptroller and Auditor General specially calls attention to the fact that on the journeys to Hatfield there has been a regular charge of 2s. for porterage and 5s. for a fly from the station to the house, although the distance is only about two-thirds of a mile."

Mr. Sparks, who had the good fortune to be employed in the office of Director of Public Prosecutions for about four years, when his place was abolished, has obtained from the Treasury a pension for life of £187 15s. per annum.

An excess of £1,330 9s. 7d. was charged to the public last year for fees on the creation of peers, of which fees a large proportion goes to the Garter-King-at-Arms. Mr. Arthur O'Connor asked:

"Take Lord Wolseley's case. That will do as a fair specimen. Why cannot they make Lord Wolseley a viscount, or a duke, or anything else they choose, without putting the public to the expense of £755 2s.?—Part of it is due to other people's pockets, the heralds', and part of it is due by Act of Parliament to the exchequer. This part of the fee is in the nature of a tax.

"But why should it go into the pockets of the heralds at the public expense?—Because they have a vested interest in some of the fees.

"Who creates the heralds?—I think it is the Duke of Norfolk, the Earl Marshal.

"Then he can give a permanent interest in the perpetuation of the peerage?—I suppose so."

Colonel Kingscote, examined before the Public Accounts Committee, said:

"Lady Willoughby de Eresby is the Hereditary Chamberlain of the Lordship of Strathearn, and under an old Royal Charter she receives £15 a year; she receives other payments for the Crown, but she receives £15 from the Crown as payment for collecting the duties of Strathearn, which amount to about £116 a year. It is an hereditary office over which we have no control."

£1,453 worth of tinware for the use of troops on voyage was left in the hands of Messrs. Henderson Brothers, the owners of the vessel, "because they were not worth the carriage to Deptford". This sum of £1,453, representing entirely tin articles, was absolutely lost.

Secret Service.

In 1877 there were two items, one of £10,000, charged on the Consolidated Fund, and the other of £24,000, in the Civil Service Estimates, for Secret Service Money. The first item of £10,000 has been erased from our national expenditure, but the £24,000 has increased to £50,000.

The House of Commons ought to insist on the nation knowing whether this amount is disbursed at home or abroad. If the sum is only paid to supplement official salaries, it should be voted openly. If it is employed for bribery, or in pursuance of dishonest work, it should not be voted at all. It is probable that a considerable portion of the £50,000 is expended in connexion with the attempts at detection of political offenders and dynamiting criminals, but there is no reason why the exact total of the amount so expended should not be explicitly stated. Each minister who expends, or through whom secret service money is expended, should at any rate each year have the total he expends distinctly associated with his name. About 250 years ago the House of Commons committed a Secretary of State to the Tower for refusing to give information as to the alleged disposal of Secret Service Moneys, and the House only released the, at first, obstinate offender on his making full submission and furnishing complete accounts. To-day the House of Commons is too subservient to Ministers to do anything half so bold.

The need for any "secret service" money is hardly clear, when the evidence taken before the Public Accounts Committee (1906) shows "In the expenditure under 'Special Missions' a sum of £1,875 given as a bribe to the Prime Minister of the Rajah of Tenom". This appears to have been given for an unsuccessful endeavor to obtain the release of the "Nisero" captives. Secret service money is expended without any audit, and Sir W. Dunbar, the Comptroller and Auditor-General, says :

"The only reason hitherto brought forward in justification of departmental resistance to the Law of Parliament is, that if proofs of the application of secret service money were placed in the hands of the Comptroller and Auditor-General, such a course might possibly admit him to a knowledge of some of the purposes covered by the vote which, in the interests of the public service, should be kept undivulged. In my judgment, though a plausible, it is by no means a convincing reason for evading the clear requirements of the Exchequer and Audit Departments Act. Secret service money, when disbursed, must of necessity pass through many hands; and why should the same trust, which is and must be reposed in subordinate officers, not be extended to the Comptroller and Auditor-General, who is a high Parliamentary functionary, holding one of the most responsible offices under the Crown, and is therefore bound by every obligation of duty and honor to act with discretion and without reproach? It may be safely assumed that, so far from revealing anything which would be compromising to the interests of the State, the only items in the secret service account which he is likely to challenge publicly would be payments, if any such occur, which have been applied to other than secret service purposes."

And Mr. Hamilton, C.B., and Mr. Ryan, C.B., in answer to the Public Accounts Committee, say (1168): "It is perfectly possible that if the Comptroller and Auditor-General objects to a payment on an open vote, because it seems to him a wrong one, a person distributing secret service money may discharge it from secret service money; we cannot tell that".

We now come to the items for superannuations, retired allow-ances, and gratuities for charitable and other purposes, or, in plain words, to the Pension List.

We who are Radicals do not object to pensions given for real service; nor do we object to large pensions if the service rendered to the nation has been equivalent. The retiring pensions to our common law and chancery judges are generally well, sometimes even hardly, earned, and none of them should be grudged. We do object to all pensions corruptly obtained or granted without equivalent national service; we object especially to hereditary pensions, and we contend that Parliament has the right to cancel an improperly received pension without having either the legal or moral obligation to make any compensation to the deprived pensioner.

The subject of Perpetual Pensions has been exhaustively

dealt with by the Select Committee on Perpetual Pensions, who report:

"1. That pensions, allowances, and payments ought not in future to be granted in perpetuity, on the ground that all such grants should be limited to the persons actually rendering the services intended to be rewarded by such grants, and that such rewards should be wholly or in main part defrayed by the generation benefited by the services so recognised. That it is unjust that future generations should be burdened with payments to persons who have had no share in the original services.

"2. That offices with salaries and without duties, or with merely nominal duties, ought to be abolished.

"3. That all existing perpetual pensions, allowances, and payments, and all hereditary offices, should be determined and abolished.

"4. That in all such commutations the Lords of the Treasury should take into consideration the circumstances of the origin of such pension, allowance or payment, and whether or not any real service had been rendered by the original grantee, or was now performed by the actual holder, of the office.

"5. That where no service, or merely nominal service is rendered by the holder of an hereditary office, and where no service or merely nominal service, was rendered by the original grantee of the pension, allowance, or payment attached to such office, the pension, allowance, or payment shall in no case continue beyond the life of the present holder or recipient.

"6. That in all cases the method of commutation ought to involve and ensure a real and substantial saving to the nation.

"7. That the rate of commutation usually adopted, of about 27 years' purchase is too high."

The Select Committee also reported:

"That since the 1st January, 1881, 330 pensions, payments, and allowances, amounting in all to the annual sum of £18,957 9s. 6d., have been commuted by the payment of £527,933 18s. 4d., and at rates of commutation varying from 10 years to 30 years' purchase.

"That some of these pensions appear to have been commuted, notwithstanding formal objections in writing lodged with the Lords of the Treasury, and without sufficient inquiry into the matters stated in such objections."

The following Perpetual Pensions still remain uncommuted:

Duke of Richmond, £19,000; Duke of Grafton, £6,870; Lord Mayor and citizens of Dublin, £724 11s. 8d.; Under Librarian at Marsh's Library, St. Patrick's, Dublin, £26 2s.

8d. ; Marquis of Downshire, for rent of ground near Carrick-
fergus Castle, £13 18s. 4d. ; University of Aberdeen, £320 ;
University of St. Andrew's, £630 ; University of Edin-
burgh, £575 ; University of Glasgow, £707 ; King's Inn
Library, Dublin, £433 6s. 8d. ; Sion College, £363 15s. 2d. ;
Duchy of Lancaster, Annuity in lieu of Prisage and Butlerage
on Wines, £803 ; Duchy of Cornwall, compensation for loss of
duties on the coinage of Tin, £16,216 15s. ; Heritable Usher of
Scotland, now payable to Hugh James Rollo for the Trustees
of the late Miss Mary Walker, £242 15s. ; Duke of Hamilton,
Hereditary Keeper of the Palace, Holyrood House, £45 10s. ;
Viscount Exmouth, £2,000 ; Earl Nelson, 5,000 ; Duke of
Grafton as Officer of the Pipe, payable to R. Harrison, £62 9s.
8d. ; Lord Rodney, £2,000 ; Sir Edward Hulse, £10 4s. 6d. ;
owner of Cheshunt Park, now payable to F. J. Prescott and
others, £26 15s. ; Master of the Hawks, payable to the Duke
of St. Albans, £965 ; Lord of the Liberty of Furness, now payable to E. Wadham, £9 ; Heirs of Thomas Warren, now payable
to Georgiana M. Archer, £12 7s. 2d. ; A rent resolute issuing
out of the Castle of Fillingharne now payable to the trustees
and executors of the late Earl of Dysart, £75 10s. ; Dauver-
querque, Seignor, Henry de Nassau, now payable to L. L.
Cohen, £375 16s. ; Constable of the Fort of Hillsborough, now
payable to the Marquis of Downshire, £216 13s. 4d.   University of St. Andrew's : Donation to the United College, £140 ;
Professor of Hebrew, £25 ; Professor of Ecclesiastical History,
paid to the Principal of St. Mary's College, £150 ; Bursar, £30.
University of Edinburgh : Professor of Ecclesiastical History,
£100 ; two Bursars, at £25 each, £50.   University of Aberdeen : King's College, £193 6s. 8d. ; Mareschal College, £86
13s. 4d. ; Two Bursars, at £10 each, £20.   Glasgow University :
Professor of Civil Law, £90 ; Professor of Physic, £40 ; Pro-
fessor of Church History, £100 ; Professor of Oriental Lan-
guages, £15 11s. 1d. : Professor of Physics, £8 6s. 8d. ; Pro-
fessor of Ethics, £8 6s. 8d. ; Professor of Logic, £2 17s. 9d. ;
Professor of Greek, £5 ; Professor of Humanity, £8 6s. 8d. ;
Professor of Divinity, £16 13s. 4d. ; Professor of Botany, £100 ;
Principal of the College, £38 4s. 5d. ; three Bursars, at £10
each, £30 ; three Bursars, at £13 6s. 8d. each, £40.   Precentor
of the Town Church, St. Andrew's, £5 11s. 1d. ; Precentor of
the Town Church, Glasgow, £5 ; Precentor of the Town Church,
Dumfermline, £5 11s. 1d. ; Minister of Queensferry, £21 ;
Minister of Brechin, £21 5s. 6d. ; Minister of the Gaelic Chapel,
Cromarty, £50 ; Minister of Lerwick, £27 15s. 6d. ; Minister
of Dunkeld and Dowally, 43 bushels 3 pecks of meal, and 43
bushels 3 pecks of barley, payable at the Fiars prices of the
county.   Perpetual Curate of Alderney, £90 ; Perpetual Curate
of Alderney, in consideration of the relinquishment of the

Fish Tithes, £5. The Master and Fellows of Gonville Hall and
Caius College, Cambridge, £2 14s. 4d. ; The Master and Fellows
of Trinity College, Cambridge, £18 12s.; University of Cam-
bridge (perpetuity) £8 3s. 2d. ; for a Preacher of the University
of Cambridge, £8 3s. 6d. ; for a Professor of Divinity of the
University of Cambridge, £11 5s. 2d. ; for a Professor of Law
of the University of Cambridge, £34 18s. ; for a Professor of
Physic of the University of Cambridge, £34 18s.; Emmanuel
College, Cambridge, £14 3s. 4d. Eton College, Provost and
Fellows, £36 13s. 9d. Dean and Chapter of Christchurch,
Oxford, £20 1s. 6d. ; for Poor Scholars of Oxford University,
£3 1s. 6d. ; for a Preacher of the University of Oxford, £7 19s.
6d. ; for a Professor of Divinity of the University of Oxford,
£11 5s. 2d. ; for a Professor of Law of the University of Oxford,
£34 18s. ; for a Professor of Physic of the University of Oxford,
£36. Creation money payable to the Bursar of Trinity College,
Cambridge, for the Counties of Cambridge and Hunts, £5 6s.
8d. Corporation of Berwick, for repairs of Bridge, £90 9s.
Earl of Derby, Thomas Cholmondley and William Banck, to
be distributed among the incumbents and schoolmasters of the
Isle of Man, now payable to the Bishop of Sodor and Man,
£89 9s. Compensation for the loss of the privilege of printing
and vending almanacks : payable to Oxford University, £500;
payable to Cambridge University, £500. Mary, widow of
Richard Pendrell, and Richard Pendrell's heirs, £100; William
Pendrell and his heirs, £100; John Pendrel and his heirs,
100 marks; Humfry Pendrell and his heirs, 100 marks : George
Pendrell and his heirs, 100 marks; Elizabeth Yates and her
heirs, £50.

A huge and avoidable increase of the superannuation vote
takes place by the pensioning of men, often in the prime
of life, on the abolition of their offices, or on what is called
reorganisation. Such men should really be transferred to
other employments, and should not be allowed to thus
swell the non-effective vote. This contingency should be
made a condition of employment. It might be well
enacted—following the teaching of Joseph Hume—that
no servant of the State should be entitled to any pension
unless injured in the service of the State, and that every
employee should be paid such fair wage as, with due
economy, would enable him to make provision against
sickness and old age. The following are some few instances
of such pensioners, taken haphazard from this year's
estimates, with the date in each case of the abolition
of the office :

Sir C. A. Woods, Colonial Department, 46 years of age,

£666 13s. 4d., from the 1st April, 1857. Martin T. Wood, consul, St. Domingo, aged 42, £400, from 17th June, 1864. George Moore, consul, Richmond, aged 54, £462 10s., from 9th September, 1863. A. R. C. Johnston, aged 38, secretary and registrar superintending, China, £600, from 25th September, 1852. C. Burrows, aged 48, county court registrar, £297 16s. 8d., from 1st October, 1856. There are several other county courts registrars from same date. G. Wilkins, examiner of criminal prosecutions, £550, from 1st April, 1877. F. G. Wheeler, aged 45, second-class clerk, £125, from same date.

Here are a few samples from the Foreign Office:

F. B. Alston, chief clerk, age 50, pension £794 2s., abolition of Foreign Office agencies, from 1st December, 1870. J. G. B. Dashwood, senior clerk, age 47, pension £601 5s., reorganisation of office, from 1st April, 1881. A. Foster, assistant book-keeper, age 38, pension £114, reorganisation of office, from 30th June, 1882. Sir E. Hertsiet, C.B., librarian, age 46, pension £349 13s. 8d., abolition of Foreign Office agencies, from 1st December, 1870. J. B. Hole, senior clerk, age 50, pension £566 13s. 4d., reorganisation, from 18th February, 1872. James W. Ridgway, Queen's foreign service messenger, age 44, pension £280, reduction, from 1st April, 1870. Earl of St. Germans, assistant clerk, age 46, pension £390, reorganisation of office, from 1st April, 1881. F. S. M. Stephens, assistant clerk, age 45, pension £400 16s. 8d., reorganisation of office, from 8th May, 1881. H. B. Wilson, translator, age 38, pension £108 6s. 8d., abolition of office, from 14th October, 1886.

Privy Council Office:

P. F. Debarry, fourth clerk, aged 43, £115, since 1st April, 1858.

The reorganisation of the Patent Office costs us in Compensation allowances:

S. Casserley, extra clerk, £116 13s. 4d., from 25th March, 1884. J. E. Docura, ditto, £99 3s. 4d., from 25th March, 1884. J. J. V. Elwin, principal, £400, from 25th March, 1884. A. C. Forrester, clerk, £250—£60 6s., from 25th March, 1884. A. P. Gipps, first class clerk, £291 13s. 4d., from 1st April, 1880. A. J. Prothero, ditto, £308 6s. 8d., from 1st April, 1880. T. A. Sims, ditto, £321 1s., 1st April, 1880. R. D. Spinks, clerk, £256 13s. 4d., from 25th March, 1884. A. Tolhausen, Ph. Dr., M.A., translator, £200, from 25th March, 1884. Total, £2,303 17s.

Compensation Allowances in connexion with the Slave Trade Commission cost:

J. Ashwood, First Clerk, Sierra Leone, age 43, pension (in

addition to pension of £51 per annum as clerk in charge,
Liberated African Department, Sierra Leone), £168 15s., cause
of retirement reorganisation, from 1st October, 1871. J. V.
Crawford, Clerk to Commissioners, Havana, age 43, pension
£173 6s. 8d., cause of retirement reorganisation, from 1st
October, 1871. A. G. Dunlop, Commissary Judge, Havana,
age 57, pension (in addition to pension of £396 13s. 4d. per
annum as late Consul and British Post Office Agent, Havana)
£100, cause of retirement abolition of office, from 1st October,
1871. S. John James, Registrar, Jamaica, age 39, pension
£132, cause of retirement abolition of office, 12th January,
1852. E. L. Layard, Judge, Cape of Good Hope, age 45,
pension (the amount of this allowance is £200, but £100 only
is payable during Mr. Layard's re-employment in the Public
Service) £100, cause of retirement abolition of office, from 21st
November, 1870. William Ryder, Arbitrator, New York, age
54, pension £200, cause of retirement abolition of office, from
1st April, 1868. Wm. Smith, Registrar, Sierra Leone, age 56,
pension £666 13s. 4d., cause of retirement abolition of office,
from 1st October, 1871. Total, £1,540 15s.

The following are Compensation Allowances for Scotch
offices, which have been all abolished:

C. Robertson, Presenter of Signatures to her Majesty in
Court of Exchequer, Scotland, age 65, £290, since 1st April,
1873.
PARTICULAR REGISTERS OF SASINES: John Allan, Keeper of
the Register for Banff, age 31, £58 12s. 10d., since 1st March,
1869. T. Hill, Joint Keeper, Renfrew and Glasgow, age 58,
£2,886 12s. 8d., since 31st March, 1871. J. McLean, Keeper,
Wigtown, age 45, £65 17s. 2d., 1st October, 1869. John
Murray, Keeper, Roxburgh, Selkirk, and Peebles, age 40,
£473 16s. 2d., since 1st October, 1869. Robert Romanes,
Keeper, Berwick, and Baillerie of Lauder, age 41, £159 16s. 11d.,
since 18th March, 1869.

The following batch of Irish Resident Magistrates
receive Compensation Allowances for the abolition and
reorganisation of their offices in October, 1882:

J. T. Butler, £522; W. L. Byrne, £134 11s. 8d.; R. C.
Coote, £311 13s. 4d.; M. Dennehy, £139 14s.; Hon. M. J.
Ffrench, £675; Sir W. F. G. Hort, £450; J. McCullagh, £450;
A. C. Montgomery, £450; W. C. Morony, £675; W. O'Hara,
£450; G. Parkinson, £366 13s. 4d.; J. W. Percy, £304 6s. 10d.;
E. C. Wynne, £236 18s. Total, £5,165 17s. 2d.

The following officers of the Order of the Bath have

been in receipt of superannuation allowances since their retirement, 1st January, 1859:

Walter A. Blount, Genealogist and Blane Coursier Herald, £124 13s. 6d.; Rear-Admiral Sir M. Seymour, as Registrar £105 19s. 8d., and as Secretary a further £158 4s. 1d.

The pensions in the Consular department are individually fairly large, and though many of them are granted on retirement for ill-health, it is not a little remarkable how long some of the sick men live to receive their pensions. Take as instances the following:

George Morison, Consul at Nagasaki, at the age of 31 retired from ill-health on 1st January, 1864, on a pension of £360; W. H. Pedder, Consul at Amoy, aged 52, on a pension of £702 3s. 2d., on 1st May, 1878; F. Parish, Consul at Buenos Ayres, aged 49, on a pension of £639 2s., on 1st February, 1874; Thomas Wood, Consul at Patras, aged 57, £583 6s. 8d., on 1st May, 1858.

This peculiarity is not confined to the Consular department:

On 1st April, 1858, C. E. Boothby, aged 37, education examiner, received, and still receives, his sick allowance of £153 6s. 8d.; Chas. Tylcote, Queen's messenger, has been in receipt of £135 sick pension since 1st August, 1843; Robert Anstruther, Home Office clerk, has been in receipt of sick allowance since 1st September, 1874.

The following are the pensions for Diplomatic Services:

A. G. G. Bonar, Minister, Berne, £900, from 24th April, 1874. J. H. Burnley, Chargé d'Affaires, Dresden, £750, from 18th October, 1873. Sir J. Crampton, bart, Envoy Extraordinary and Minister Plenipotentiary, £1,300, from 1st July, 1869. W. Doria, Secretary of Embassy, St. Petersburg, £700, from 1st August, 1877. The Right Hon. Sir H. G. Elliott, Minister, etc., Vienna, £1,700, from 16th January, 1884. Rev. R. S. Ellis, Chaplain, Copenhagen Legation, £133 6s. 8d., from 1st January, 1883. R. P. Ffrench, Envoy Extraordinary, etc., Vienna, £700, from 1st April, 1878. G. J. R. Gordon, Minister, Stuttgardt, £900, from 1st January, 1871. F. D. Hamilton, Minister Resident, Quito, £900, from 17th November, 1883. Admiral the Hon. Sir E. Harris, Minister at the Hague, £1,300, from 19th November, 1877. E. Herries, C.B., Secretary of Legation in Italy, £700, from 7th August, 1875. Sir H. Howard, G.C.B., Minister, Bavaria, £1,300, from 1st January, 1872. T. F. Hughes, Oriental Secretary, Constantinople, £700, from 12th November, 1875. Rev. G. L. Johnston, Chaplain,

Vienna, £165, from 1st April, 1885. A. Lambros, Clerk and Translator, Athens, £103 6s. 8d., from 1st July, 1878. Sir A. H. Layard, Ambassador, etc., at Sublime Porte, £1,700, from 23rd October, 1884. W. G. Lettsom, Chargé d' Affaires and Consul General, Uruguay, £900, from 29th July, 1869. Lord Augustus Loftus, G.C.B., Ambassador, St. Petersburgh, £1,700, from 9th April, 1879. Earl of Lytton, G.C.B., Envoy Extraordinary, etc., Lisbon, £730, from 9th June, 1880. R. T. C. Middleton, Minister Resident and Consul General, Venezuela, £900, from 14th December, 1878. L. Moore, Second Secretary, Constantinople, £500, from 1st October, 1877. Sir Charles A. Murray, Envoy Extraordinary, etc., Lisbon, £1,300, from 10th October, 1874. Count A. B. S. Pisani, C.M.G., Keeper of the Archives and Superintendent of the Chancery, Constantinople, £750, from 1st January, 1878. J. G. F. Russell, Secretary, Copenhagen, £500, from 23rd October, 1879. D. E. Saurin, Secretary, Washington, £700, from 1st October, 1885. General Sir E. Stanton, Chargé d' Affaires, Munich, £900, from 12th February, 1882. R. Stuart, Minister Resident, Hayti, £580, from 1st May, 1883. Sir Thomas F. Wade, K.C.B., Minister in China, £1,300, from 1st July, 1883. R. G. Watson, Secretary, Stockholm, £500, from 1st January, 1880. Sir C. L. Wyke, G.C.M.G., K.C.B., Minister, etc., Lisbon, £400, from 21st February, 1884. (Also receives £900 per annum from Consolidated Fund.) £25,581 13s. 4d.

The following are pensions to Colonial Governors :

Sir H. Barkly, Governor, Cape of Good Hope, £1,000, from 31st March, 1877. Sir G. Berkeley, K.C.M.G., Governor, Leeward Islands, £417 10s., from 27th June, 1881; he also receives £240 from Colonial funds. Colonel G. A. K. D'Arcy, Governor, Falkland Islands, £333 6s. 8d., from 1st May, 1876. E. J. Eyre, Governor, Jamaica, £750, from 24th February, 1874. Sir S. Freeling, K.C.M.G., Governor, Trinidad, £663 6s. 5d., from 1st January, 1885. Colonel Sir T. Gore Browne, Governor, Bermuda, £750, from 22nd April, 1871. Sir George Grey, Governor, New Zealand, £1,000, from 14th, April, 1872. K. B. Hamilton, Governor, Antigua and Leeward Islands, £500, from 5th July, 1865. Sir R. W. Harley. K.C.M.G., C.B., Lieutenant-Governor, British Honduras, £333 6s. 8d., from 26th March, 1884. Colonel Sir S. J. Hill, K.C.M.G., C.B., Governor, Newfoundland, £750, from 1st May, 1876. Sir C. H. Kortright, K.C.M.G., Governor, British Guiana, £1,000, frcm 17th April, 1882. Sir J. R. Longden, G.C.M.G., Governor, Ceylon, £1,000, from 10th July, 1883. A. W. Moor, President, St. Kitts, £272 6s. 8d., from 10th May, 1883. Major Mundy, R.M., Lieutenant-Governor, British Honduras, £333 6s. 8d., 18th March, 1877. Marquess of Normanby,

G.C.M.G., P.C., Governor, Victoria, £1,000, from 18th April, 1884. Sir B. C. C. Pine, K.C.M.G., Governor, Natal, £750, from 10th April, 1875. Sir R. W. Rawson, Governor, Windward Islands, £232 8s. 9d., from 31st May, 1875 ; in addition to £395 per annum from the Government of the Cape of Good Hope, and £477 12s. 7d. from the Government of Mauritius. Sir John Scott, K.C.M.G., Governor, British Guiana, £1,000, from 27th December, 1873. Sir P. E. Wodehouse, Governor, Cape of Good Hope, £725, from 13th March, 1881 ; in addition to £275 from the Government of Ceylon.

We still pay as part of the pensions to the Household of the late King of the Belgians :

Edward Kobert, gamekeeper, £75 ; Charles Moore, head steward, £95 10s., both since 11th December, 1865.

Sir F. Sandford—retired, three years ago, from the Education Office, on account of age, on a pension of £1,333 6s. 8d.—is now appointed Under-Secretary for Scotland, at a salary of £1,500, and is also allowed £500 on account of his pension.

In a speech delivered at a Conservative *fête* at Whitby on September 23rd Lord Randolph Churchill said :

" I think we may fairly look for great reductions of public expenditure and great reforms in our public services and public departments. What is the general character of the public services of this country at the present moment ? It is this—the great feature and characteristic of it is this, and it is one of which you may well be proud—that we employ three men to do the work of one—(laughter and cheers)—and we pay each of the three men at least one third higher salary than you need pay to one man who would do the work which the three pretend to do. (Renewed laughter and cheers.) We retire three men prematurely on high pensions at a time when they are perfectly capable of doing great service to the State. That is the general feature and characteristic of the public services of Great Britain generally, supposed to be the most practical country in the world. And I particularly allude to the pension list, because the pension list of this country has reached proportions which make it positively nothing short of a national scandal. (Cheers.) The pension list of this country is a list amounting to, I believe, over six millions of money a year; six millions of money in mere pensions ; 3d. in the income-tax, imagine what that is ! With those six millions, in about forty years you might pay off the whole of the National Debt, which costs you twenty-six millions a year at the present moment. This gives you an idea of the pressure of the pension list upon the people,

and of what vital importance it is that the pension list should
be cut down and kept down. (Cheers.) But to go back to
your public services. If the State purchases articles for its
own use by contract, it generally pays from 20 to 40 per cent.
more than a private individual would do. (Hear, hear.) If
the State thinks it will manufacture the articles it wants for
itself by itself, the cost of manufacturing is about double what
the private manufacturer would incur. (Hear, hear.) These
are no mere assertions—they have been proved over and over
again by speeches, committees, and inquiries of all sorts and
kinds—they are undeniable facts; and with all this ludicrous
and shameful extravagance in public expenditure, it is admitted
by all, at the same time, that you have not real efficiency in
your public services and your public departments. Well, I do
not know whether you agree with me, but I am strongly of
opinion that the time for this state of things has gone by.
(Cheers.)"

Revenue Departments.

The cost of collection of our customs and inland revenue
might be much lessened if direct taxation were made the
rule. Almost all earnest financial reformers seek to substitute direct for indirect taxation. Indirect taxation is a levy
of revenue by taxes on the transit of merchandise, on
articles of food, on the raw materials used in manufacture,
and on the process of manufacture. Direct taxation is here
intended to mean the levy of revenue by a tax on income.
There are, of course, various direct taxes of obnoxious
character which would be utterly impolitic. Indirect taxation is objectionable, because, in the end, the pressure of it
always falls most severely on the mass of the consumers,
and the richer taxpayers manage to transfer their burdens
with interest to the poorer and ultimate purchasers. Indirect
taxation is always a hindrance to industrial enterprise. It
encourages smuggling, fraud, and perjury, and compels the
maintenance of a strong force for the detection and punishment of the crime it creates. The governing classes, and
those who are opposed to economy, will naturally object to
direct taxation, for its very simplicity makes each taxpayer
unpleasantly and immediately conscious of every increase
in his fiscal burdens. Almost all local taxes are direct
taxes, and when all imperial taxes are direct there will
be less opportunity of annual increase in our expenditure
without a vigorous protest. Men and women ought to

pay taxes for the preservation of their property, their
liberty, and their persons, but the severest pressure of tax
ought not to come upon those whose wage is insufficient
for the decent maintenance of themselves and their families.
In 1849 the Liverpool Financial Reform Association issued
some most able tracts dealing with the questions of direct
and indirect taxation. Since that date very many indirect
taxes have been entirely abolished, but there is still enough
of indirect taxation remaining to make the following
passage worth reproducing from the Financial Reform
Tract, No. 3 :—

"On a careful examination of the sources whence the public
income is derived, the Association are astonished to find how
completely the taxation is laid on the trade and industry of
the country. Contrasted with the accounts of the expenditure,
it divides the community into two distinct classes: one, those
who pay; the other, those who spend the taxes. The former
comprises the great mass of the population, all who labor and
produce the wealth of the nation; the other, the favored few
who from accident of birth or connexions are exempt from the
necessity of toil; and who seem on that account (for no other
reason can be discovered in the examination of official documents,
but the fact that such is the exemption) to be relieved from
the duty of contributing their fair and proportionate amount
to the pecuniary requirements of the State."

It is, of course, just to add that—thanks to men like
Joseph Hume, John Bright, Richard Cobden, and last but
most certainly not least, William Ewart Gladstone—much
change for the better has been made since 1849 in the
imposition of our national taxation.

Post Office.

The Post Office is looked to as a source of revenue in
aid of taxation, and there is each year a constant surplus
of revenue over expenditure. In 1876 the surplus was
£2,534,306; in 1877, £2,504,461; in 1878, £2,693,666;
in 1879, £2,917,656; in 1880, £2,890,488; in 1881,
£3,239,109; in 1882, £3,248,704; in 1883, £3,287,307;
in 1884, £2,901,404; in 1885, £2,931,728; in 1886,
£2,987,343; in 1887, £2,639,107. I venture to doubt
whether the financial conduct of the Post Office should be
regarded as for a surplus in aid of revenue. The

work of the Post Office should be done at such rate that
those who use it should bear the cost proportionally to
their uses, but the rate for carrying letters, parcels, and
telegrams should be made as low as can be without loss,
so as to facilitate intercommunication. In some of the
higher branches of the Post Office and Telegraph Service
there is room for economy; but the lower class employees
are very wretchedly paid, and, considerable temptations
coming in the way of the poorest, there is a large conse-
quent crime, which might possibly be avoided.

The True Principle of Taxation.

The true principle of taxation should be, that every
member of the State who earns or possesses, or receives
more than is necessary for the mere subsistence of himself
and his family, should contribute towards the national
taxation in due proportion to his ability to pay, and to his
stake and interest in the nation. It is submitted that at
present the main source of revenue from taxes in the
United Kingdom is the earnings of the laborer, and that
even the burden of the income tax, assessed taxes, and
other taxes, which seem to fall exclusively, or principally,
on the richer classes, are really ultimately borne almost
entirely by the producing classes.

All taxes direct and indirect, paid by the producers or
importers of commodities, or paid by the dealers therein,
and all taxes direct and indirect incurred on the productions of land, must in the end be paid by the consumers of
house commodities and productions. Taxes originally paid
to the tax collector by the producer or importer of any
commodity, and by the traders and dealers therein, are all
repaid by the ultimate consumer in the augmented price
of the article he purchases.

Taxation of Land and Income.

It has been suggested that a graduated land tax might
be imposed so as to press very severely upon unduly large
landed estates, thus preventing the continuance of the
enormous aggregations of land in the hands of a compara-

tively few owners, of which we have some very glaring instances in this densely populated country. About 10,888 persons own 51,885,118 acres of land in the United Kingdom, and 2,238 of these persons own no less than 39,924,432 acres. One duke amongst these owns 1,208,666 acres. It is also suggested that a special land tax operating as a penalty tax should be imposed on all land held in an uncultivated (that is, an unutilised) state. This would either force large quantities into cultivation, or compel its abandonment by the present owners. In such case of abandonment the land might become vested in the local authority, with power to let to tenant cultivators under such conditions as would afford facilities and encouragement for the reclamation and cultivation of such lands. It is further suggested that a like graduated tax should be applied to all inherited incomes above a certain amount.

How Expenditure should be checked.

At present, though the estimates are presented to Parliament at the beginning of the Session, there is no certainty of any real or effective criticism of any of the votes, unless some individual member happens by good luck to have special knowledge. The chief effort by private members in discussion on estimates is generally to raise some point of complaint against particular individuals whose salaries are included in a vote. Much time is therefore often occupied with discussion on grievances which, though fit to be brought before Parliament, have only a very remote relation to economy in outlay, and ought really to be raised by separate motion before the Speaker leaves the chair. In the Session of 1887, as the Government took the whole time, such proper Parliamentary course was impossible, and private members had only the opportunity afforded in Committee on the estimates. To ensure reasonable and methodical investigation, I suggest that at the commencement of each Session separate small select committees—say of three or five members each—be appointed for each class of votes in the Civil Service, one select committee each for army, navy, post-office, and revenue services. That the votes should not be taken in committee of supply until the small select committee had examined the permanent official by whom the estimate had been prepared, and, if necessary, the minister responsible for the vote. The committee of the whole House would then have before it, with the estimate, the evidence, and any report of the small select committee on the vote. The evidence taken before the Public Accounts Committee and the Appropriation Accounts, only throw light on money which has been already expended. What is really needed is such information as may determine the necessity for, or prevent, the expenditure. The Opposition, or independent members below the gangway on each side, and especially on the Radical side, ought to arrange beforehand for the proper criticism of the estimates in Committee of Supply by allotting special items to be spoken upon by the best fitted men. At present the criticism is uncertain, and the attack guerilla-like. There ought also to be reasonable certainty as to when particular classes and votes will come on for discussion. In this 1887 Session the same votes were on the paper night after night for five or six weeks without being reached, and were ultimately hurried through unexpectedly in the haste which, towards the close of the Session, is the re-action against a wearying delay.

The following is the Account of the Public Income and Expenditure of the United Kingdom of Great Britain and Ireland for the year ended 31st March, 1887, as published in compliance with sec. 4 of the Act 38th and 39th Vic., cap. 45.

INCOME.

	£	s.	d.	£	s.	d.
CUSTOMS				20,155,000	0	0
EXCISE				25,250,000	0	0
STAMPS (excluding Fee, etc., Stamps)				11,830,000	0	0
LAND TAX and HOUSE DUTY				2,980,000	0	0
PROPERTY and INCOME TAX				15,900,000	0	0
POST OFFICE				8,450,000	0	0
TELEGRAPH SERVICE				1,830,000	0	0
CROWN LANDS (Net)				370,000	0	0
INTEREST on Advances, Local Works, Cape Railway, etc.	997,246	3	8			
INTEREST on Purchase Money of Suez Canal Shares	178,946	3	11	1,176,192	7	7
MISCELLANEOUS :						
Allowance out of the Profits of Issue received from the Bank of England, per Act 24th Vict., cap. 3	153,895	0	0			
Net Profit, Post Office Savings Banks	64,608	15	11			
Fee, etc., Stamps	714,038	10	3			
Other Miscellaneous Receipts	1,899,023	4	2	2,831,565	10	4
TOTAL INCOME				£90,772,757	17	11

EXPENDITURE.

	£	s.	d.	£	s.	d.
PERMANENT CHARGE OF DEBT:						
INTEREST (except as below) and Management of the Debt..	18,976,657	8	10			
Terminable Annuities	8,131,217	13	0			
Interest on Exchequer Bills	88,075	15	11			
Interest on Treasury Bills for Supply	67,610	13	7			
Interest on Bank Advances (Deficiency)	17,492	8	1			
Interest on Bank Advances (Ways and Means)	1,640	8	2			
	27,282,694	7	7			
Trustee Savings Banks, Deficiency Annuity	83,672	12	0			
				27,366,366	19	7
INTEREST, etc., on Treasury Bills, etc. (Loans for Local Purposes, including Cape Railway, etc.)				391,711	15	10
INTEREST, ETC., ON SUEZ EXCHEQUER BONDS				199,944	0	0
OTHER CHARGES ON CONSOLIDATED FUND:						
Civil List	410,065	8	2			
Annuities and Pensions	345,517	14	0			
Salaries and Allowances	89,182	12	0			
Courts of Justice	500,431	9	8			
Miscellaneous Charges	304,828	6	6			
Friendly Societies Deficiency	20,000	0	0			
Localisation of the Military Forces	73,866	0	0			
				1,743,891	10	4
Carried forward......				29,701,914	5	9

Brought forward .... £ 29,701,914 s. 5 d. 9

SUPPLY SERVICES:
Army (including Army Purchase) 18,429,271 15 9
Navy 13,265,401 8 4

(The growth of the Naval and Military Expenditure on the peace establishment has been as follows: 1876, £25,199,761; 1877, £25,488,430; 1878, £25,065,129, but in this year there were extra services amounting to £3,500,000 on the Russo-Turkish Vote of Credit; 1879, £25,763,531—this year the extra services, Russo-Turkish war, South Africa, and Abyssinia, amounted to £4,485,829; 1880, £25,251,032, and extra, chiefly for South Africa, £3,245,487; 1881, £24,625,602, but the Transvaal and Afghan expeditions swallowed also £1,156,000; 1882, £24,997,498, with £2,404,500 added for Transvaal, Zululand, and Afghanistan; 1883, £25,376,357, with £4,409,500 for Egypt, Transvaal, and Afghanistan; 1884, £26,450,578, with £1,381,750 for Egypt and Afghanistan; 1885, £27,014,002, with £3,563,000 for Bechuanaland, Egypt, and Afghanistan; 1886, £29,833,993, with £9,701,000 Vote of Credit and Afghanistan; 1887, £31,918,139. These figures, from Parliamentary Paper 301, printed 26th August, 1887, slightly vary from the Finance Accounts of each year.)

Miscellaneous Civil Services 17,826,453 16 9

(The Miscellaneous Civil Services in 1876 cost £12,731,053; in 1877, £12,745,198; in 1878, £13,368,791; in 1879, £14,281,892; in 1880, £14,447,459; in 1881, £14,935,430; in 1882, £15,469,281; in 1883, £16,363,126; in 1884, £16,255,817; in 1885, £16,637,300; in 1886, £16,867,863; in 1887, £17,206,198. Of course, the larger part of the great increase in these services during the past seventeen years has been in Class IV., Education, Art, and Science, which is this year £5,484,470 as against £1,545,232 in 1869–70, when we initiated the great change.)

Customs and Inland Revenue Departments 2,676,918 6 6
Post Office 5,436,892 9 2
Telegraph Service 1,935,000 0 0
Packet Service 724,900 0 0
————— 60,294,837 16 6

TOTAL EXPENDITURE in the year ended 31st March, 1887 .. £89,996,752 2 3
776,005 15 8

Excess of Income over Expenditure £90,772,757 17 11

CATALOGUE OF WORKS

SOLD BY THE

Freethought Publishing Company,

63, FLEET STREET, LONDON, E.C.

JANUARY, 1888.

WORKS

SOLD BY THE

FREETHOUGHT PUBLISHING COMPANY,

63, FLEET STREET, LONDON, E.C.

————◆————

Bradlaugh, Charles—*(See also International Series.)*

The Freethinker's Text-Book. Part I.—1. "The Story of the Origin of Man, as told by the Bible and by Science." 2. "What is Religion?" "How has it Grown?" "God and Soul." Cloth, 2s. 6d.

Impeachment of the House of Brunswick.—Ninth edition. 1s.

Theological Essays. Bound in cloth, 3s.

Political Essays. Series I. contains: Impeachment of the House of Brunswick; Real Representation of the People; John Churchill, Duke of Marlborough; Mr. Gladstone or Lord Salisbury; Five Dead Men whom I knew when living; Cromwell and Washington, The Land, the People, and the Coming Struggle. Bound in cloth, 2s. 6d. Series II. contains: Taxation; The Channel Tunnel; The Radical Programme; Compulsory Land Cultivation. In paper cover, 1s.

The Parliamentary Struggle, containing the whole of the documents. Cloth, 1s.

Socialism. Containing the written Debates with Annie Besant and E. Belfort Bax, and "Socialism: its fallacies and dangers". In paper cover, ... 1 0

DEBATES—All Verbatim Reports.

Four—with the Rev. Dr. BAYLEE, in Liverpool; the Rev. Dr. HARRISON, in London; THOMAS COOPER, in London; the Rev. R. A. ARMSTRONG, in Nottingham; with Three Discourses by the BISHOP OF PETERBOROUGH and Replies by C. BRADLAUGH. Bound in one volume, cloth, 3s.

What does Christian Theism Teach? Two nights' Public Debate with the Rev. A. J. HARRISON. 6d.

God, Man, and the Bible. Three nights' Discussion at Liverpool with the Rev. Dr. Baylee. 6d.

BRADLAUGH, CHARLES (*continued*)—

God as the Maker and Moral Governor of the Universe. Two nights' Discussion with THOMAS COOPER. 6d.

Has Man a Soul? Two nights' debate at Burnley, with the Rev. W. M. WESTERBY. 1s.

Christianity in relation to Freethought, Scepticism, and Faith. Three Discourses by the BISHOP OF PETERBOROUGH, with Special Replies. 6d.

Secularism Unphilosophical, Unsocial, and Immoral. Three nights' debate with the Rev. Dr McCANN. 1s.

Is it Reasonable to Worship God? Two nights' debate at Nottingham with the Rev. R. A. ARMSTRONG. 1s.

Will Socialism benefit the English People? One night's debate with H. M. HYNDMAN. 3d.

Socialism: For and Against. Written debate with Annie Besant. 4d.

Will Socialism benefit the English People? Written debate with E. Belfort Bax, 6d.

PAMPHLETS— *s.*

Taxation: how it originated, how it is spent, and who bears it. 2nd Edition. Completely revised to date .. 0 6

The Channel Tunnel: ought the Democracy to support or oppose it? 0 2

Notes on Christian Evidences. In reply to the Oxford House Papers, with rejoinders by the Rev. E. S. Talbot, M.A., Rev. Francis Paget, D.D., W. Lock, M.A., T. B. Strong, B.A., Rev. V. S. S. Coles, M.A. 0 6

Compulsory Land Cultivation.. .. .. .. 0 3

Socialism: its fallacies and dangers 0 2

Lying for the Glory of God: a letter to the Rev. Canon Fergie (Wigan) 0 1

Supernatural and Rational Morality 0 1

England's Balance-Sheet for 1886. 16 pp. 0 1

Letter to Lord Randolph Churchill, M.P., Chancellor of the Exchequer. 16 pp. 0 1

Mr. Gladstone or Lord Salisbury: which? An appeal to the Electors. 12 pp. 0 1

The Radical Programme 0 2

What Freemasonry is, what it has been, and what it ought to be 0 2

The True Story of my Parliamentary Struggle. Containing a Verbatim Report of the proceedings before the Select Committee of the House of Commons; Mr. Bradlaugh's Three Speeches at the Bar of the House, etc., etc. .. 0 6

Fourth Speech at the Bar of the House of Commons .. 0 ½

May the House of Commons Commit Treason? .. .. 0 ½

BRADLAUGH, CHARLES (*continued*)—   *s. d.*

Verbatim Report of the Trial, The Queen against Bradlaugh and Besant. With Portraits and Autographs of the two Defendants. Second Edition, with Appendix, containing the Judgments of Lords Justices Bramwell, Brett, and Cotton. Cloth, 5s.

Splendid large-sized Photograph of Charles Bradlaugh, mounted for framing, 5s. Cabinet Photograph of C. Bradlaugh, 2s.

BRADLAUGH, CHARLES (*continued*)—

Bust of C. Bradlaugh, half life-size, 5s. ; packed in box for safe carriage, 5s. 6d.

Chromo-litho of Charles Bradlaugh. Cabinet size, 1d. ; in Letts's protecting case, post free, 2d. Large size, 6d. ; in Letts's protecting case, post free, 7d.

Litho portrait of C. Bradlaugh, fit for framing, large size, 6d. ; in Letts's protecting case, 7d. Mounted, in black and gold frame, 5s.

Besant, Annie—

The Freethinker's Text-Book. Part II. "On Christianity." Section I.—"Christianity : its Evidences Unreliable." Section II.—"Its Origin Pagan." Section III.—"Its Morality Fallible." Section IV.—"Condemned by its History." Cloth, 3s. 6d.

History of the Great French Revolution. First Series, cloth, 2s. Second Series, 9d. Third Series, 9d. One vol., cloth, 3s. 6d.

My Path to Atheism. Collected Essays. Cloth, gilt lettered, 4s.

Light, Heat, and Sound. Illustrated. In three parts, 6d. each. Cloth, 2s.

The Jesus of the Gospels and The Influence of Christianity on the World. Two nights' Debate with the Rev. A. HATCHARD. 1s.

Social and Political Essays. 3s. 6d.

Theological Essays and Debate. 2s. 6d.

Legends and Tales (*Young Folks' Library*). Legends :—1. Ganga, the River Maid. 2. The Stealing of Persephone. 3. The First Roses. 4. The Drowning of the World. 5. A Curious Adventure. 6. Drawn from the Waters. 7. The Wandering Jew. Tales :—1. Hypatia. 2. Giordano Bruno. Cloth, attractively bound, illustrated, 1s.

Autobiographical Sketches. With Cabinet Photograph. Uniform with "International Library". 4s.

Disestablish the Church, or Sins of the Church of England. A *Vade Mecum* for Liberationists, full of details about Tithes, "Church" Revenues, Persecuting Laws, attitude of the Church towards education, the slavery question, etc., etc. Prettily bound in cloth, gilt lettered, with Index of Contents, 1s.

Atheism and its bearing on Morals. Written Debate with Rev. G. F. Handel Rowe, of Halifax, 6d.

The Teachings of Christianity. Written Debate with Rev. G. F. Handel Rowe, of Halifax, 6d.

Is Socialism Sound? Four Nights' Debate with G. W. Foote. Cloth, on heavy paper, 2s. Paper covers, 1s.

Essays on Socialism. Cloth, 2s. 6d.

Socialism : For and Against. Written debate with Charles Bradlaugh, 4d.

Roots of Christianity, or The Christian Religion before Christ 0 6

Life, Death, and Immortality 0 2

BESANT, ANNIE (*continued*)—

s. d.

PAMPHLETS—

	s.	d.
The World and its Gods	0	3
A World without God. Reply to Miss F. P. Cobbe	0	3
Woman's Position according to the Bible	0	1
Christian Progress	0	2
Fruits of Christianity. Fifth Thousand	0	2
The Gospel of Christianity and the Gospel of Freethought	0	2
Blasphemy	0	1
The Christian Creed. Parts I. and II., each	0	6
God's Views on Marriage	0	2
The Gospel of Atheism. Fifth Thousand	0	2
Why I do not **believe** in God	0	3
Is the Bible Indictable?	0	2
Biblical Biology	0	1
What is the Use of Prayer? Tenth Thousand	0	1
The Myth of the Resurrection. Tenth Thousand	0	1
Why should Atheists be Persecuted?	0	1
The True **Basis** of Morality. A Plea for Utility as the Standard of **Morality.** Seventh Thousand	0	2
The Ethics of Punishment	0	1
Sin and Crime: their nature and treatment	0	3
The Natural History of the Christian Devil	0	1
Is Christianity a Success?	0	1
Sins of the Church. In 8 numbers, each (16 pp.)	0	1
Do. do. Cloth, with index	1	0
Do. do. Part I. (6 numbers)	0	6
Auguste Comte. Biography of the great French Thinker, with Sketches of his Philosophy, his Religion, and his Sociology. Being a short and convenient *résumé* of Positivism for the general reader	0	6
Giordano Bruno, the Freethought Martyr of the Sixteenth Century. His Life and Works	0	1
The Law of Population Its consequences, and its bearing upon Human Conduct and Morals. 130th thousand	0	6
Social Aspects of Malthusianism	0	1
Legalisation of Female Slavery in England	0	1
The Physiology of Home—No. 1, "Digestion"; No. 2, "Organs of Digestion"; No. 3, "Circulation"; No. 4, "Respiration"; 1d. each. Together, in neat wrapper	0	4
Electricity and its Modern Applications. Four lectures. 1d. each. Together, in wrapper	0	4

8

BESANT, ANNIE (*continued*)—

Eyes and Ears	0	3
Vivisection	0	1
Modern Socialism	0	6
Why I am a Socialist	0	1
Radicalism and Socialism	0	3
The Socialist Movement (Reprinted from *Westminster Review*)	0	3
The Evolution of Society	0	3
The Redistribution of Political Power	0	4
Gordon judged out of his own mouth	0	2
Liberty, Equality, and Fraternity	0	1
Landlords, Tenant Farmers, and Laborers	0	1
The English Land System	0	1
English Marseillaise, with Music	0	1
English Republicanism	0	1
The Political Status of Women. A Plea for Women's Rights	0	2
Civil and Religious Liberty, with some Hints taken from the French Revolution. Sixth Thousand	0	3
The Transvaal	0	1
England's Jubilee Gift to Ireland	0	1
Force no Remedy. An analysis of the Coercion Act (Ireland) 1882	0	1
Egypt, a Protest against the War. Second Edition	0	2
The Story of the Soudan	0	1
Free Trade *v.* "Fair" Trade—No. 1, "England before the Repeal of the Corn Laws"; No. 2, "The History of the Anti-Corn Law Struggle"; No. 3, "Labor and Land: their burdens, duties, and rights"; No. 4, "What is really Free Trade?" No. 5, "The Landlords' Attempt to Mislead the Landless". In neat wrapper with Appendix	0	6
Large Photograph of Annie Besant, for framing	10	6
Cabinet ditto	2	0

New Cabinet, 6d. P. 1d. Per doz., 4s. 6d. P. 6d.

Anderson, Geo., C.E.—
Address to Working Men's Institutes. 16 pp. in wrapper, 2d.

Atheistic Platform, Parts I. and II., 6d. each. Parts I and II. in wrapper together, 1s. In Penny Numbers: 1. "What is the Use of Prayer?" By Annie Besant. 2. "Mind considered as a Bodily Function." By Alice Bradlaugh. 3. "The Gospel of Evolution." By Edward Aveling, D.Sc. 4. "England's Balance Sheet." By Charles Bradlaugh. 5. "The Story of the Soudan." By Annie Besant. 6. "Nature and the Gods." By Arthur B. Moss. 7. "Some Objections to Socialism." By Charles Bradlaugh. 8. "Is Darwinism Atheistic?" By Charles Cockbill Cattell. 9. "The Myth of the Resurrection." By Annie Besant. 10. "Does Royalty Pay?" By George Standring. 11. "The Curse of Capital." By Edward Aveling, D.Sc. 12. "Why should Atheists be Persecuted?" **By Annie** Besant.

Aveling, Edward B., D.Sc., Fellow of Univ. Coll., London.— *(See also International Series.)*
>Essays, limp cloth, 1s. General Biology, cloth, 2s. Physiological Tables, 2s. Botanical Tables, 1s. Bookworm, 1s. The Value of this Earthly Life, **1s.** Biological Discoveries **and** Problems, 1s. Science and Secularism, 2d. Science and Religion, **1d.** Superstition, 1d. Wickedness **of** God, 1d. Irreligion of Science, 1d. God dies : Nature remains, **1d.** A Godless Life the Happiest and Most Useful, **1d.** Sermon on the Mount, **1d.** Darwinism and Small Families, **1d.** Religious Views of Darwin, 1d. The Gospel of Evolution, 1d. The Curse of Capital, 1d. Plays of Shakspere, **4d.** Macbeth, **4d.**

Ball, W. P.—
>The Ten Commandments, **1d.** Religion in Board Schools, 2d.

Bastiat, Frederic—
>Popular Fallacies regarding Trade and Foreign Duties. **Adapted** to the Present Time by Ed. R. Pearce. Boards, 79 pp., **6d.**

Baxter, W. E.—Our Land laws of the past, 3d.

Beauchamp, P. (G. Grote, the historian of Greece)—
>Analysis of the Influence of Natural Religion on the Temporal Happiness of Mankind. 123 pp. 1s.

Blackie, Prof.—Jewish Sabbath **and** Christian Lord's Day, 2d.

Blanchard, J.—Essays and Addresses, **1s.**

Bonser, T. O., M.A.—The Right to Die, 1d.

Bradlaugh, Alice—Mind **considered as a** Bodily Function, 1d.

Bradlaugh Bonner, Hypatia—
>Princess Vera, and other Stories (*Young Folks' Library*). Contains:—Princess Vera ; A Day's Adventures ; How the World was Made ; Tommy and I ; A Children's Picnic. Cloth, prettily bound, illustrated, 1s.
>Four Lectures on The Chemistry of Home : Air, I., Air, II., Water, I., Water, II., 1d. each , or in wrapper, 4d. Four Lectures on The Slave Struggle in America. 1d. each, **or in** wrapper, 4d. Secular Education, 7½d. per 100, post free.

Brodrick, Hon. George—Reform of English Land System, 3d.

Buchner, Prof. Ludwig, M.D.—*(See also International Series.)*
>The Influence of Heredity on Free Will. Translated from the German by Annie Besant. 2d.

C. B. X.—Aurora. A story. 6d.

Cattell, Charles C.—The Age of the Earth, etc. A reply to Sir J W. Dawson. 2d. Is Darwinism Atheistic ? 1d.

Christ and Osiris. 2d.

Cobden, Richard—The Three Panics, 1s.

Cobden's Political Writings. Cloth, 704 pp. 6s.

Conway, Moncure D.—*(See also List B.)*
Liberty and Morality. 3d.

Cooper, Robert—
Holy Scriptures Analysed. With Life by C. Bradlaugh. 6d.

Corner, Our. Edited by Annie Besant. Vol. I., Jan. to June;
Vol. II., July to Dec., 1883; Vol. III., Jan. to June; Vol
IV., July to December, 1884; Vol. V., Jan. to June; Vol. VI.,
July to December, 1885; Vol. VII., Jan. to June , Vol. VIII.,
July to December, 1886; Vol. IX., Jan. to June, 1887; Vol. X.,
July to December, 1887; handsomely bound, cloth gilt, 3s. 6d.
each. Christmas Number, 1883, 6d. Yearly subscription, post
free, 7s. A monthly Freethought and Radical magazine.

Courtney, Herbert L.—The House of Commons, Past, Present,
and Future, 4d. Secular *v.* Christian Morality, 1d. The New
Gospel of Hylo-Idealism, or Positive Agnosticism, 3d.

Crisis in Farming, The; its Radical Causes and their only
Remedies. Twenty-two evils arising from Landlord, thirteen from
Tenant. By the Author of "Hints to Landlords and Tenants". 6d.

Crofts, W. R.—City Missionaries and Pious Frauds, 1d.

Dalton, H. R. S., B.A., Oxon.—
The Education of Girls, Second Edition, 6d. Ish's Charge to
Women, 4d. Religion and Priestcraft, 2d.

D., E.—To be, or not to be? (On future existence.) $\frac{1}{2}$d.

Drysdale, C.R., M.D.—
The Population Question, 1s. Tobacco, and the Diseases it Pro-
duces, 2d. Alcohol, 6d. Animal Vaccination, 6d.

"Eastern Traveller"—Fables of Faith, 3d.

Ellershaw, Charles—
The Soil of Great Britain and Ireland. In neat wrapper, 6d.

Ellis, Ellen—Everything is possible to Will. A most useful Temperance Story. Cloth, 3s. 6d.

Elmy, Ben W.—The Cause of Woman. From the Italian of Louisa
To-Sko. 6d. Studies in Materialism, 4d.

Farrar, Sir T. H., Bart.—Free Trade *v.* Fair Trade (3rd edition).
376 pp., Crown 8vo, cloth, 2s. 6d.

Forlong, Major-Gen. J. G. R., F.R.G.S., F.R.A.S., &c.—
Rivers of Life, or Sources of Streams of the Faiths of Man in all
lands; showing the Evolution of Faiths from the rudest sym-
bolisms to the latest spiritual developments. With maps, illustrations, and separate chart of faith streams. In 2 vols. quarto,
cloth gilt, £6 6s.
A Colored Chart of all Faith Streams, 7½ feet by 2¼ feet, folded
in case, or on rollers, £1 6s. P. 6d.

Garrison, Prof. H. D.—The Absence of Design in Nature, 2d.

Haeckel, Prof. Ernst (*See International Series*).

Headingley, A. S.—
Biography of Charles Bradlaugh. With Appendix by W. Mawer (revised and enlarged). Cloth, 2s. 6d.

Hindu, A—Reflexions on the Blasphemy Prosecutions, 2d.

Holt, R. B.—
Utile Dominium, or The Right to Use the Land, 8 pp., demy 8vo, 1d. *Absolutum et directum Dominium*, or Absolute Ownership of Land. 8 pp., demy 8vo, 1d.

Holyoake, G. J.—
New Ideas of the Day, 1d.

Howell, Constance—
Biography of Jesus Christ, 1s. ; cloth gilt, 1s. 6d. The After-Life of the Apostles, 1s. ; cloth gilt, 1s. 6d. History of the Jews, 1s., cloth gilt, 1s. 6d. Written for Young Freethinkers. The cloth edition is tastefully bound in uniform style.

"Humanitas"—
Is God the First Cause? 6d. Bound in cloth, with other Essays, 1s. 6d. Socialism a Curse, 3d. Thoughts upon Heaven, 6d Charles Bradlaugh and the Oath Question, 2d. How C. Bradlaugh was treated by the House of Commons, 2d. Charles Bradlaugh, M.P. and the Irish Nation, 6d. Jacob the Wrestler; paper, 2s. ; cloth, 2s. 6d. A Fish in Labor, or Jonah and the Whale, 3d.

Hume, David—
On Miracles, 3d. With appendix, etc., by J. M. Wheeler.

Hunter, W. A., M.A.—Past and Present of the Heresy Laws. 3d.

"Indian Officer"—
The True Source of Christianity ; or, a Voice from the Ganges Originally published at 5s. Paper covers, 1s. ; cloth gilt, 1s. 6d.

Ingersoll, Col. Robert—
Library Edition : Oration on the Gods, 6d. Oration on Thomas Paine, 4d. Heretics and Heresies, 4d. Oration on Humboldt, 2d. Arraignment of the Church, 2d. These can be supplied in one volume, neatly bound in limp cloth, 1s. 6d. Mistakes of Moses, 3d. Liberty of Man, Woman and Child, 6d. Modern Thinkers : or, the Spirit of the Age, 1d. Hell, 2d. Decoration Day, 1d. Salvation, 1d. Ingersoll at Home, 1d. Prose Poems, 2d. Tilt with Talmage, 1d.
Popular Edition, 16 pages, 1d. each : 1. Take a Road of Your Own ; 2. Divine Vivisection, or Hell ; 3. The Christian Religion ; 4. The Ghosts, Part I. ; 5. The Ghosts, Part II. ; 6. Thomas Paine the Republican. In wrapper, 6d. 7. Is all of the Bible inspired ? Part I. ; 8. Is all of the Bible inspired ? Part II. ; 9. Mistakes of Moses ; 10. Saviors of the World, 11. How Man makes Gods ; 12. Law, not God. From 7 to 12 in wrapper, 6d. The 12 in wrapper, 1s. 13. What Must I Do to be Saved? Part I. ; 14. What Must I Do to be saved ? Part II. ; 15. The Spirit of the Age ; 16. Human Liberty ; or, Intellectual Development, Part I. ; 17. Human Liberty ; or, In-

tellectual Development, Part II.; 18. Which Way? From 13 to 18, in wrapper, 6d.

International Library of Science and Freethought—
Mind in Animals, by Professor Ludwig Büchner. Translated, with the author's consent, by Annie Besant, 5s.
The Student's Darwin, by Edward B. Aveling, D.Sc. (Lond.) Fellow of University College (Lond.), etc., price 5s.
Jesus and the Gospels, and The Religion of Israel, by Jules Soury, 4s.
Genesis: its authorship and authenticity, by C. Bradlaugh. 5s.
The Pedigree of Man, and other Essays (illustrated with 80 woodcuts), by Dr. Ernst Haeckel, translated from the German, with the author's consent, by Edward B. Aveling, D.Sc. 6s.

Irving, William—
Charles Bradlaugh as a Politician, Social Reformer, and Thinker. In paper cover, 4d.

"Julian"—
Natural Reason *versus* Divine Revelation. An appeal for Freethought. Edited by Robert Lewins, M.D. 6d.

"Justice"—Peace and Prosperity. An Essay on Social Questions, with remedies for existing evils. 6d.

Kay, Joseph—
Free Trade in Land. With Preface by John Bright, 1s.

L. W. H.—The House of Lords. 1d.

Land Law Reform League Leaflets, No. 1 to 6 in assorted packets for distribution, 6d. per 100; post free, 7½d.; an assorted dozen, 1½d.

L'Estrange, Thos.—The First Seven Alleged Persecutions, A.D 64 to A.D. 235. 6d. The Eucharist, 6d.

Levy, J. Hyam—
Wealthy and Wise. A Lecture introductory to the Study of Political Economy. 6d.

Lewins, Robert, M.D.—
Humanism *versus* Theism, or Solipsism (Egoism) = Atheism, 6d.

Local Government and Taxation of the United Kingdom,
520 pp., cloth, with index, 5s., containing a series of essays:—
Local government in England, by the Hon. G. C. Brodrick; County boards, by C. T. D. Acland; Areas of rural government, by Lord E. Fitzmaurice; London government, and how to reform it, by J. F. B. Firth; Municipal boroughs and boundaries, by J. T. Bunce; Local government and taxation in Ireland, by R. O'Shaughnessy; Local government and taxation in Scotland, by W. Macdonald; Local taxation in England and Wales, by J. Roland Phillips.

Major, A.—A Few Objections to Spiritualism, 2d.

"Materialist"—
A Reply to Cardinal Manning's Essay on "The Relation of the Will to Thought", 3d.

Mawer, W.—
The Latest Constitutional Struggle. Being a Diary of the North-ampton Struggle from April 2nd, 1880. 2d. Reasons why Blasphemy Prosecutions should be abolished. 2d.

Medley, G. W.—England under Free Trade, 3d.

Mitchell, Logan—
Religion in the Heavens; or, Mythology Unveiled. In a Series of Lectures. Cloth, 2s. 6d.

Mongredien, A.—Free Trade and English commerce, 6d.

Montague, F. C.
The Old Poor Law and the New Socialism, or Pauperism and Taxation. 6d.

Moss, Arthur B.—
Nature and the Gods, 1d. Man and the Lower Animals, 1d. 16 pp., each.

Murray, D.—
Is Knowledge sufficient to prevent Crime? 1d.

National Reformer—Index to, 1883, 1884, 1885, 1886, 2d. each. Cases for loose numbers, with holding-cords, 2s.

National Secular Society's Almanack for 1882, 1883, 1884, 1885, 1886, 1887, and 1888. 6d. each. P. 1d. each.

"Neptune"—Our Naval Policy, 1d.

One hundred and one Questions. 1d.

Paine, Thomas—*(See also List B)*.
Common Sense. With new Introduction by C. Bradlaugh. 6d.
The Age of Reason. With Preface by C. Bradlaugh. 1s. Cloth, 1s. 6d.
Rights of Man. With Introduction by C. Bradlaugh. 1s. Cloth gilt, 1s. 6d.
Theological Works; including the "Age of Reason", and all his Miscellaneous pieces and Poetical Works; his last Will and Testament, and a Steel Portrait. Cloth, 3s.

Parable of Modern Times, A. 2d.

Paul, Alexander—History of Reform, 1s.

Pearce, E. R.—Popular fallacies on trade and foreign duties, 6d.

Peers and the People, The, an appeal to history, 1d.

Perot, J. M. A.—Man and God. Cloth, 4s.

Robertson, John M.—
Royalism, 4d. Socialism and Malthusianism, 2d. Toryism and Barbarism, 2d. The Upshot of Hamlet, 6d.
Sins of the Church, Nos. 9—14, "The Perversion of Scotland", 1d. each; or in 1 vol., cloth, with index, 9d.

"S. S."—
Unscientific Religion; or, Remarks on the Rev. J. M. Wilson's "Attempt to treat some Religious Questions in a Scientific Spirit". In paper cover, 4d.

Salmon, C. S.—
Crown Colonies of Great Britain. Stiff boards, 184 pp. 1s.

Sins of the Church ; A series of pamphlets. 16 pages each, 1d.
Nos. 1 to 4: "Threatenings and Slaughters" [England]; 5 and 6: "For the Crown and against the Nation"; by Annie Besant. No. 7: "A Burden on Labor"; No. 8: "The Church a Creature of Crown and Parliament," by Annie Besant; Nos. 9—14 "The Perversion of Scotland," by John Robertson.
Nos. 1 to 8, in cloth, with index, etc., 1s. ; Nos. 9 to 14, in cloth, with index, 9d.
Part I. (Nos. 1 to 6 in wrapper), 6d. Part II. (Nos. 7 to 12 in wrapper), 6d.

Soury, Jules (*See International Series.*)

Standring, George—
Life of C. Bradlaugh, with portrait and autograph, 12 pages, 1d. Life of Colonel R. G. Ingersoll, with portrait and autograph, and extracts from his orations, in wrapper, 1d. Court Flunkeys ; their Work and Wages, 1d. Does Royalty Pay ? 1d.

Symes, Jos.—
Christianity essentially a Persecuting Religion, 2d. Hospitals and Dispensaries not of Christian Origin, new and revised edition, 1d. Christianity and Slavery, 2d. Christianity at the Bar of Science, 3d. Atheistic Despair, 2d. Debate on Atheism with Mr. St. Clair, 1s. Debate and eight essays, bound, cloth, neat, 3s.

Three Trials of William Hone, The, for Publishing Three Parodies, viz., The late John Wilkes's Catechism, The Political Litany, and The Sinecurists' Creed ; on three ex-officio informations, at Guildhall, London, during three successive days—December 18th, 19th, and 20th, 1817—before three special juries and Mr. Justice Abbot, on the first day, and Lord Chief Justice Ellenborough, on the last two days. 2s.

Thursday Lectures at the Hall of Science—
Containing Mr. Bradlaugh's lectures on Anthropology, Annie Besant's on The Physiology of Home, Hypatia Bradlaugh's on The Chemistry of Home, and Dr. Aveling's on The Plays of Shakspere. Complete in one vol. Cloth, 2s.

Torrens, Sir R.—Transfer of land by Registration under method operative in British Colonies. 6d.

Volney, C. F.—(*See also List B.*)
Ruins of Empires, with Plates of Ancient Zodiac, cloth, 2s.

Wheeler, J. M.—
Frauds and Follies of the Fathers. 6d.

Young Folks' Library ; edited by Annie Besant. Cloth, boards, attractive binding, illustrated —
I. Legends and Tales, by Annie Besant, 1s.
II. Princess Vera, and other Stories, by H. Bradlaugh Bonner. 1s.

LIST B.

SPECIAL LIST OF REMAINDERS.

All at the lowest price, no reduction to the trade, **the**
object being to supply readers of the "**NATIONAL
REFORMER**" with literature at specially low **rates.**
Order must be accompanied by cost of postage, **which**
is inserted after the letter P. Where **no postage is**
mentioned, the goods go by rail at cost of purchaser,
and 2d. in addition to price must be sent for booking.

Adam, W.—

First Lessons in Geology. With special article on the Toadstones
of Derbyshire, a glossary explanatory of geological terms and
derivations, with sections, and general diagram of strata. 173
pp., paper covers (published at 1s. 6d.), 3d. Post free 4d.

Theories of History, with special reference to the principles of
the Positive Philosophy. Favorably noticed by J. S. Mill.
Demy 8vo., 441 pp., 3s. P. 4½d.

Agassiz, Louis—On Classification. 8vo. Pp. vii. and 381. Cloth
(published at 12s.), reduced to 3s. P. 4½d.

Alexander, J. E., Lieut.-General—

Cleopatra's Needle, the Obelisk of Alexandria. Cloth, 8vo., 109
pp (published at 2s. 6d.), 1s., post free.

Alison, Alex.—The Philosophy and History of Civilisation.
Cloth, royal 8vo., 478 pp., 2s. **P. 4½d**

Anti-Papal Library, The.—"Mary Alacoque and the worship
of the Sacred Heart of Jesus, presented in their real character,"
by Louis Asseline. Published at 4d. Post free 1½d. "Confession in the Church of Rome: what it is and what it does." By
the noted writer, M. Morin. (Published at 1s.) 80 pp. 3d. P. 1d.
These pamphlets are translated by the celebrated Unitarian, Dr.
J. R. Beard, and are full of information concerning the frauds
and impostures of the Romish Church.

"Antipodes."—The Revelations of Common-sense. Crown 8vo.,
pp. xi. and 452. 2s. P. 4½d.

Argyll, Duke of—
Causes of the Afghan War, being a selection of the papers laid before Parliament, with a connecting narrative and comment. 8vo, cloth, 326 pp. (published at 6s.), 1s. 6d. P. 4½d.

Bain, Professor Alexander, LL.D.—
James Mill. A biography. With portrait. Cloth, 8vo, 466 pp., 2s. 6d. P. 4½.

Bale, G. G. P.—Anatomy and Physiology of Man. School edition Profusely illustrated (published at 7s. 6d.), 2s. 6d. P. 4½d.

Barratt, Alfred—
Physical Ethics, or the Science of Action. Contents: Axioms, Definitions, Propositions, Moral Sense, Human Development, Unselfish Emotions, Individual Development, Will, Obligation, Pleasures that are called Bad, Rearrangement, Systems which make Good a Primary Quality, Systems which offer an Explanation of the Nature of Good, Theological Systems, Organisation of Moral Systems, Objections of inutility of falsehood, of sneers, Mr. Spencer's Doctrine of the Absolute, Laws of Mental Redistribution, Perception of Time, Motion, and Space; Relation of Mind to Matter, Æsthetic Emotions, Religion of Positivism, Theological Basis of Morality. Cloth, crown 8vo, 387 pp., 2s. (pub. at 12s.). Postage 4½d.
Physical Metempiric. Contents: Definitions, The Physical Method, Other Consciousness, Things-in-themselves, The Atomic Theory, Monads, Time and Space, Noumena and Phænomena, Monadism and Monism, Physical Evolution, Existence, Mental Evolution, General Theory of the Relation of Mind and Matter, Objections, The "Suppression" of Egoism, Ethics and Politics, Ethics and Psychogony. With Portrait of the Author. Cloth, 8vo, 311 pp., 2s. (Published at 12s. 6d.) P. 4½d.

Benvenuti, B. F.—
Episodes of the French Revolution, from 1789 to 1795, with an appendix embodying the principal events in France from 1789 to the present time, examined from a political and philosophical point of view. Demy 8vo, 310 pp., 1s. 6d. P. 4½d.

Berkeley, Bishop—
* The Principles of Human Knowledge. Treatise on the nature of the Material Substance (and its relation to the Absolute), with a brief introduction to the doctrine and full explanations of the text; followed by an appendix, with remarks on Kant and Hume, by Collyns Symons, LL.D. 1s. P. 3d.

Bernard, H. H., Ph.D.—
Lessing on Bibliolatry. 144 pp. (published at 5s.), 1s. 6d. P. 3d.

Black, C., M.D.—
On the more evident changes the body undergoes, and the management of health from infancy to adult age. Cloth, 138 pp. (published at 2s. 6d.), 6d. P. 2d.

Blake, Carter, D.Sc.—
Zoology for Students. With Preface by Professor Owen. Profusely Illustrated. Cloth. 382 pp. 3s. 6d. P. 4½d.

Bonaparte, Napoleon (Jerome)—
Clericalism in France. Translated by Annie Besant. 3d., post free.

Boyle, F.—
Savage Life. Notes in South Africa, A Night in Granada, Philosophy of the Angle. Cloth, demy 8vo, 332 pp., 3s. P. 4½d.

Bradlaugh, Charles—
Hints to Emigrants; containing notes of employment, wages, costs of living, &c., personally made during three journeys in the United States of America. (Published at 1s.) Post free, 6d.

Brittlebank, W.—
Persia during the Famine: a narrative of a tour in the East, and the journey out and home. Cloth gilt, 8vo, 265 pp., 1s. P. 4½d.

Brown, W.—
The Labor Question. Paper Currency and Lending on Interest as affecting the prosperity of Labor, Commerce, and Manufactures. Cloth gilt, 240 pp. (published at 2s. 6d.), 6d. P. 3d.

Bryce, Arch. H., LL.D., &c.—
Second Latin Book. Readings, with notes, from Cæsar, Ovid, &c., with Syntax and copious Vocabulary. Crown 8vo, 422 pp., 1s. P. 3d.

Buchner, Prof. Ludwig—
Force and Matter. 284 pp. (published at 5s.), 2s. 6d. P. 3d.

Burke, Edmund—The inherent evils of all State Governments demonstrated. 66 pp. (published at 1s.), 3d. P. 1d.

Burton's Prairie Traveller; or, Overland Route.—With map, illustrations, and itineraries of the principle routes between the Mississippi and the Pacific. By General RANDOLPH MARCY. Crown 8vo, pp. 270, cloth, reduced to 1s. 6d. P. 3d.

Bushby, Rev. Edward, B.D.—Essay on Human Mind, with Elements of Logic. 84 pp., in stiff wrapper, 3d. P. 1d.

Butler, J., LL.D.—
The Analogy of Religion, Natural and Revealed, to the constitution and course of Nature. To which are added two brief dissertations: I. Of personal identity; II. Of the nature of virtue. With index and questions for examination by the Rev. G. B. WHEELER, A.M., Cloth, gilt, pp. 350, 2s. 6d. P.4½d.

Caird, J.—British Land Question. 2d. P. 1d.

Campbell, Sir George, M.P.—
White and Black; the outcome of a visit to the United States. Cloth 8vo, 440 pp., 2s. 6d. P. 6d.

Cant-Wall, E., Barrister-at-Law—
Ireland under the Land Act, with an appendix of leading cases under the Act, giving the evidence in full, judicial dicta, etc. 8vo, 280 pp., cloth (published at 6s.), 1s. 6d. P. 4½d.

Cattell, Charles C.—The Coming Republic (published at 2s. 6d.), 1s. 6d.; P. 3d. Republicana, 244 pp., 6d.; P. 2½d. Sunday Lectures on Science and Freethought, 157 pp., 1s.; P. 1½d.

Challice, John, M.D.—
Medical advice to mothers on the management of children in health and disease. Limp cloth, 98 pp., 3d. P. 1d.

Chastel, E., Professor—
Christianity in the Nineteenth Century. A Religious and Philosophical Survey of the Immediate Past. Translated by J. R. Beard. Cloth, crown 8vo, 236 pp., 1s. P. 3d.

Clifford-Smith, J. L.—
Social Science Association. A Narrative of Results. With admirable photographs of Lord Brougham and G. W. Hastings, M.P. Cloth, 190 pp., published at 2s. 6d., offered at 6d. P. 2d.

Cobden, Richard—Biography by J. E. Ritchie. With superb steel engraving, 4d. P. 1½d.

Coleridge, Samuel Taylor—
Letters, Conversations, and Recollections. With preface by the Editor, Thomas Allsop. Cloth 250 pp., 2s. P. 3d.

CONTEMPORARY REVIEW.—1874, complete in 2 vols., 5s. (published at 15s. each); containing articles by W. E. Gladstone, Sir T. Brassey, Sir W. Herschell, Professor Clifford, Dean Stanley, Karl Blind, and many other famous writers.

And these numbers, 3d. each :—1875. January contains Supernatural Religion (The Silence of Eusebius), by Prof. Lightfoot; Sermon on the Immutability of Jehovah, by Colenso; Max Müller's reply to Darwin; Saxon Studies, by Julian Hawthorne, etc., etc. March contains Saturn and the Sabbath of the Jews, by R. A. Proctor; Some Results of the Challenger Expedition, by Prof. Huxley; Life at High Pressure, by W. R. Greg; On Objections to "Literature and Dogma", by Matthew Arnold, etc., etc. April contains A Jesuit Father on Papal Infallibility; The Covenanters, Charles II. and Argyle; Instinct and Reason, by St. George Mivart; Bogies of To-day, by Earl Pembroke, etc., etc. July contains Is the Church of England Worth Preserving? by W. E. Gladstone; George Jacob Holyoake on Co-operation; The Tory Party and the Catholics, by Pope Hennessey; Animal Instinct in its relation to the Mind of Man, by the Duke of Argyll, etc., etc. September contains A Discussion on the Scientific Basis of Morals between Prof. Clifford, Frederic Harrison, and P. C. W.; Lord Blachford on Huxley's Hypothesis that Animals are Automata; Ocean Circulation, by Dr. W. B. Carpenter; Right use of a Surplus, by W. R. Greg, etc., etc. November contains India, Political and Social, by M. E. Grant Duff; Religious and Conservative Aspects of Positivism, by Frederic Harrison; Liknesses, or Philosophical Anatomy, by St. George Mivart, etc., etc. The above seven numbers for 1875 free for 2s. 9d.——1876. January contains The Fallacies of Testimony, by W. B. Carpenter; Why have Animals a Nervous System? by H. Charlton Bastian; Goethe and Minna Herzlieb, by Andrew Hamilton; Wesleyan Methodism, by J. L. Davies, Public Education, by Sir John Lubbock, etc., etc. March contains Modern Materialism, by the Rev. James Martineau; Irrigation Works and the Permanent Settlement in India, by J. Dacosta; Bishop Butler, by Matthew Arnold; Eternal Perdition and Universalism from a Roman Catholic Point of View; Religion of Positivism, by Mark Pattison, etc., etc. April contains Russian Idylls, by W. R. S. Ralston; The Bases of Morals, by James Hinton; Homerology, by W. E. Gladstone; John H. Newman: a Psychological Study, by the Rev. John Hunt; Jellyfish Theory of Language, by the Rev. A. H. Sayce, etc., etc. May contains Humanity, by Frederic Harrison; Strauss: a Chapter in the History of Modern Religious Thought, by the Rev. A. M. Fairbairn; Religious Teaching in Elementary Schools, by Francis Peck, etc., etc. June contains The Courses of Religious Thought, by W. E. Gladstone; Persia, by Arthur Arnold; Evolution and the Religion of the Future, by Anna Swanwick; Elementary Education, by Sir John Lubbock, etc., etc. July contains Turkey, by Arthur Arnold; Christian Evidences, by Richard H. Hutton; Homerology, by W. E. Gladstone; The Pulse of Europe, by M. E. Grant Duff; The Restitution of all Things, by Andrew Jukes, etc., etc. September contains Automatism and Evolution, by Dr

Charles Elam; Capital Punishment in England, by Francis W. Rowsell; Church-manship of John Wesley, by James Rigg, D.D., etc., etc. October contains Imper-fect Genius: William Blake, by H. G. Hewlett; Professor Cairnes on Value, by W. T. Thornton; Antagonism of Creeds, by Philip Schaff, D.D.; Working Men and the Eastern Question, by Geo. Potter and Geo. Howell, etc., etc. November contains Philosophy without Assumptions, by Cardinal Manning; The Prophetic Element in the Gospels, by W. R. Greg; Russian Policy in Turkestan, by W. E. Glad-stone; A Psychological Parallel, by Matthew Arnold, etc., etc. The above nine numbers for 1876 free for 4s.——1877. February contains: Evolution and the Vegetable Kingdom, by W. Carruthers, F.R.S.; Problems of Social and Political Life in France, by A. Oer; The English People in relation to the Eastern Question, by Edward A. Freeman; Henrietta Maria; The Roman Catholics and the Puritans, by Peter Bayne; Transcendentalism in England, New England, and India, by H. Holbeach, etc., etc. March contains: Pro-gress of Religious Thought in Scotland, by Principal Tulloch; Race and Language, by E. A. Freeman; Spinoza: the man and the philosopher, by Arthur Bolles Lee, Prussia in the Nineteenth Century, by Prof. J. S. Blackie; Reason-able Faith, by a London Merchant, etc. April contains: Spinoza: 1677—1877, by Ernest Renan; Metaphysical Study, by Prof. Bain; The Germ Theory and Spon-taneous Generation: Pasteur, Tyndall, Bastian; One per Cent., by Prof. Bonamy Price, etc., etc. May contains: Contest of Heathenism with Christianity, by Prof. Zeller; Conditions and Prospects of the Church of England, by Thos. Hughes; Wagner, by Rev. H. R. Haweis; French Thought and Spinozism, by Paul Janet; Harriet Martineau's account of herself, by H. S. Richardson; A Reconciling Philosophic Conception, by Prof. Bain, etc., etc. July contains: Morality in Politics, by the Duke of Argyll; Pascal and Montaigne, by John Grote; Religious Upheaval in Scotland, by William Wallace; Drifting Light Waves, by R. A. Proctor; Virgil, by Julia Wedgwood, etc., etc. September contains: The Gospel according to St. John, by Ernest Renan; The Pantheistic Factor in Christian Thought, by the Rev. R. F. Littledale; Scientific Movement and Literature, by Edward Dowden; French Chateaux of the Renaissance, by Mrs. Mark Pattison (Lady Dilke), etc., etc. October contains: The Divine Guidance of the Church, by the Bishop of Salisbury; Trial of Jesus Christ, by A. Taylor Innes; Trades Unions, Apprentices and Technical Education, by George Howell; Oxygen in the Sun, by R. A. Proctor; Legislation for the Insane, by Dr. D. Hack Tuke, etc., etc. November contains: The Resurrection of Christ a new revelation, by Canon West-cott; War-Power, by Prof. F. W. Newman; Fashionable Farces; Prof. Tyndall's Birmingham address, by George Peard; The Slaveowner and the Turk, by Goldwin Smith. The above eight numbers of 1877 free for 2s. 9d.——1878. January contains: Dog Poison in Man, by Dr. Acland; J. S. Mill's Philosophy Tested, by Professor Jevons; Disestablishment, by the Duke of Argyll; The Little Health of Ladies, by Frances Power Cobbe; China, England, and Opium, by Justice Fry, etc., etc. February contains: Max Müller on the Origin of Reason, Our Indian Em-pire, by Sidney James Owen; The Provinces before the French Revolution, by H. Taine; What is in store for Europe, by Kossuth, etc., etc. June contains Facts of Indian Progress, by Monier Williams; Determinism and Moral Freedom, by Paul Janet; Scottish Influence on English Theological Thought, by D. J. Vaughan; Are the Working Classes Improvident? by George Howell; Future Punishment, Eternal Hope, by F. W. Farrar, etc., etc. July contains: The Position and Influence of Women in Ancient Greece, by Dr. Donaldson; Roman Metempsychosis: a sequel to the discussion on future punishment, by Francis Peek; Future of Judaism, by Rev. W. H. Fremantle; A curious article on a Secularist Sunday Evening, etc., etc. August contains: Max Müller on Julius Mohl; Critical Movement in the Scotch Free Church, by T. M. Lindsay; The Early Roman Baptismal Creed, by George Salmon; Parochial Charities of the City, by Walter H. James; Evolution and Pantheism, by R. St. J. Tyrwhitt.; Professor Blackie on the Scot, etc., etc. September contains: Progress of Indian Religious Thought, by Professor Monier Williams; Selling the Soul, by R. H. Horne; Life of Jesus and Modern Criticism, by Professor B. Weiss; The Sun's Corona and his spots, by R. A. Proctor; Memoir of Charles Sumner; Super-natural in Nature, etc., etc. The above six numbers for 1878 free for 2s. 6d.—— 1879. February contains: A. K. Wallace on New Guinea and its Inhabitants; Ritualism, Roman Catholicism, and Converts, by Rev. Father Ryder; Migration of Birds, by Dr. Aug. Weissman; Co-operative Stores and Common Sense, by Rev. W. L. Blackley; Contemporary Life and Thought in Russia, by T. S., St. Petersburg; Literary Chronicles, by Profs. Bonamy Price, Cheetham, S. R. Gardiner, and Matthew Browne, etc., etc. March contains: Belief in Christ: its relation to miracles and to evolution, by J. Ll. Davies; New Planets near the Sun, by R. A. Proctor; Women in Ancient Athens (Aspasia and Sappho), by James Donaldson; Confession: its Scientific and Medical Aspects, by George Cowell; New Religious Movement in France, by Josephine E. Butler, etc., etc. April contains: Carnivorous Plants, by Ellice Hopkins; Over-production, by Prof. W. S. Aldis; Bad Trade and its cause, by Stephen Williamson and R. H. Patterson; Disenclosure of the "Anglican Paddock", by J. R. Prettyman, etc., etc. May contains: The Social Philosophy and Religion of Comte, by Prof. E. Caird; Prof. St. George Mivart on the Study of Natural History; Commercial Depression and Reciprocity, by Prof. Bonamy Price; Origen and the beginning of Christian Philosophy, by Canon Westcott; Political Life in Germany, by Friedrich von Schulte, etc., etc. June contains: Conspiracies in Russia, by Karl Blind; Barbarisms of Civilisation, by Prof. F. W. Newman; British Empire in India, by J. von Döllinger; Origin of the Week, by R. A. Proctor; The New Bulgaria, by an Eastern Statesman, etc., etc. July contains: Benjamin Franklin, by Thomas Hughes; The Last Jewish Revolt, by Ernest Renan; Why is Pain a Mystery? by J. Burney Yeo; What are Living Beings? by Prof. St. George Mivart; Chloral and other narcotics, by Dr. B. W. Richardson, etc., etc. August contains: Religious Condition of Germany, by Friedrich von Schulte; Cheap Justice, by Henry Crompton; Indian Religious Thought, by Monier Williams; Progress of Education in England, by F. Peek; Conspiracies in Russia, by Karl Blind, etc., etc. September contains: The First Sin as Recorded in the Bible and in Ancient Oriental Tradition, by François Lenormant; Political and Intellectual Life in Greece, by N. Kasasis; Animals and Plants, by Prof. St. George Mivart; The Future of China, by Sir Walter H. Medhurst; Problem of the Great Pyramid, by Richard A. Proctor, etc., etc. October contains: The Supreme God in the Indo-European Mythology, by James Darmestater; Forms and Colors of Living Creatures, by Prof. Mivart; Moral Limits of Beneficial Commerce, by F. W. Newman; India and Afghanistan, by Lieut.-Col. R. D. Osborn; Myths of the Sea and the River of Death, by C. F. Keary, etc., etc. November contains: Max Müller on Freedom; The Ancient Régime and the Revolution in France, by Prof. von Sybel; The Deluge: its Traditions in Ancient Nations, by François Lenormant; What is the Actual Condition of Ireland? by E. Stanley Robertson; Suspended Animation, by R. A. Proctor, etc., etc. The above ten numbers for 1879 free for 3s. 8d.——1880. January contains: England in the Eighteenth Century, by Karl Hillebrand; Landlords and Land Laws, by J. S. Blackie; Herbert Spencer on the Data of Ethics; Relation of Animals and Plants to Time, by St. George Mivart; Philosophy in the Last Forty Years, by Hermann Lotze, etc., etc. February contains: C. B. Radcliffe on the Pedigree of Man; Geography of Living Creatures, by St. George Mivart; Forgotten Aspects of the Irish Question, by Malcolm MacColl; Usury; Contemporary Life and Thought in Turkey, etc., etc. March contains: The Vernacular Press of India, by Roper Lethbridge; Hellenic and Christian Views of Beauty, by the Rev. R. St. J. Tyrwhitt; A Sequel to the "Pedigree of Man", by Dr. Radcliffe; Duration of Parliaments, by W. R. Cassels, etc., etc. April contains: Society of the Future, by Rev. M. Kaufmann; The Genealogies between Adam and the Deluge, by F. Lenormant; Personal Property, Debt and Interest, by F. W. Newman; Relations of Living Beings to One Another, by St. George Mivart; Max Müller and Mill on Liberty; History of Rent in England, by J. E. Thorold Rogers, etc., etc. May contains: The Gospel of Evolution, by Dr. Elam; Daltonism, by W. Pole; Eleusinian Mysteries, by F. Lenormant; International Novelists and Mr. Howells, by Mrs. S. Orr, etc., etc. June contains: Mr. Ruskin's Public Letters; The French Republic and the Church, by E. Scherer; Ellice Hopkins on Ants; Greek Christian Inscriptions, by George T. Stokes; The Age of Balzac, by W S. Lilly, etc., etc. July contains: Karl Hillebrand on the Sources of German Discontent; From Faust to Mr. Pickwick, by Matthew Browne; The Indian Dilemma, by Major Grey; A Few Weeks on the Continent, by the Duke of Argyll. etc., etc. August contains: International Morality, by the Rev. J. Ll. Davies; River Water, Sea Water, and Rock Salt, by Justus Roth; Missing Millions, by Lieut.-Col. Osborn; Rent, by Prof. Bon. Price; Belgium: the Problem of Liberty in Catholic Counties, by John Rae; Comparative Æsthetics, by Vernon Lee, etc., etc. September contains: Unity of Nature, by the Duke of Argyll; Future of Canada, by George Anderson; Apprenticeship of the Future, by Prof. Sylvanus P. Thomson; Heinrich Heine, by Charles Grant, etc., etc. October contains: Man's Place in Nature, by the Duke of Argyll; Why Keep India, by Grant Allen; Through Siberia, by Rev. H. Landsdell; Theology and Materialism, by Justice Fry; Primitive Religion, by John Rae; Origin of Music, by J. F. Rowbotham, etc., etc. November contains: Animal Instinct in Relation to Mind of Man by Duke of

Argyll; Nationalisation of the Land, by A. R. Wallace; Relation of Christian Belief to National Life, by the Rev. J. Baldwin Brown; Old and New Japan, by Sir R. Alcock, etc., etc. December contains: The Duke of Argyll on the Limits of Human Knowledge; Nihilism in Russia, by Rev. J. Kaufmann; What is the House of Lords? by Prof. Bon. Price; Pusey on Everlasting Punishment; Land League and its Work, by T. P. O'Connor, etc., etc. The complete set for 1880 free for 4s. 4d.

Conway, Moncure D.—

Republican Superstitions. (Published at 7s. 6d.) 1s. 6d. P. 3d.

Human Sacrifices in England. 64 pp. (published at 1s.) 3d. P. 1d.

Demonology and Devil Lore. 2 vols., royal 8vo, with 65 illustrations (published at £1 8s.), £1. Free by parcels post, £1 0s. 9d.

Corvichen, R.—The Philosophy of all Possible Revelations.

Crown 8vo, stiff paper covers, 360 pp., 9d. P. 4½d.

Curwen, H.—A History of Booksellers, Old and New. Numerous

Portraits and Illustrations. 8vo, 483 pp., 2s. 6d. P. 4½d.

Davies, Rev. J. Ll., M.A.—

Forgiveness after Death. 40 pp., 1d. P. ½d.

Davies, Rev. Dr. Maurice—

Orthodox London. Two volumes bound in one. Contains: The Rev. H. R. HAWEIS—Father STANTON—Mr. FORREST—Rev. T. TEIGNMOUTH SHORE—Mr. LLEWELLYN DAVIES—Mr. MAGUIRE —Dean STANLEY—Canon LIDDON—Canon MILLER—Mr. STOPFORD BROOKE—Midnight Mass—Archbishop of York—Bishop of London—Bishop of Manchester—Bishop of Lincoln—etc., etc. 458 pages (published originally in Two Volumes at 28s.) 2s. 6d. P. 4½d.

Dean, J. A.—

Political Rights: How acquired, retained, or forfeited; with a sketch of such rights under ancient and modern Republics. Crown 8vo, 368 pp., cloth gilt, 1s. 6d., boards, 1s. P. 4½d.

Direy, L.—Latin Grammar. 179 pp. (published at 4s.), 6d. P. 2d.

Drew, Frederic—

The Northern Barrier of India. A popular account of the Jummoo and Kashmir Territories. With maps and illustrations. Cloth, 8vo, 336 pp. (published at 12s.), 3s. P. 4½d.

Duffield, A. J.—

Prospects of Peru. The end of the Guano Age, and a description thereof. With some account of the Guano deposits and "nitrate" plains. Cloth, 120 pp., 6d. P. 2d.

Dyas, Capt R. H.—

The Upas: a vision of the rise, reign, and decay of Superstition. Published at 10s., reduced to 2s. 6d. P. 4½d.

Eads, H. L.—Shaker Theology. 2s. P. 4½d.

Ellis, A. J.—

The Dyer's Hand; preceded by "The Way to God". Post free, 2d.

mmett's Life, 1d. Post free 1½d.

Espinasse, F.—
Voltaire : his Life and Times. 1694 to 1726. 620 pp. (published at 14s.), 2s. 6d. P. 6d.

Facts and Figures, Important events in History, Geography, Literature, Biography, Ecclesiastical History, etc., etc. Arranged in classified chronological order. Post free 6d.

Farrer, J. A.—
Crimes and Punishments. Including a new translation of Beccaria's "Dei Delitte e Delle Pene". Cloth, 8vo, 250 pp. (published at 6s.), price 1s. 6d. P. 4½d.

Fate of the Peers, The, or a few words with "Our Old Nobility". With cartoon, crown 8vo, 32 pp., 1d. P. ½d.

Frankland, Rev. B., B.A.—
The Age and the Gospel. A controversial book on the Christian side. 303 pp., 2s. P. 4½d.

Fowler, William—
Thoughts on Free Trade in Land. 8vo, 70 pp., 3d. P. 1d.

Freeman, Dr. E. A.—Political Catechism. 1d. P. ½d.

Gebler, Carl von—Galileo Galilei. 4s. P. 6d.

Giles, Rev. Dr.—
Apostolic Records of Early Christianity, from the date of the Crucifixion to the Middle of the Second Century. Cloth, new, uncut, 440 pp. Published at 8s. 3s. 6d. P. 6d.

Gladstone and Beaconsfield: whom to follow. 132 pp., 3d. P. 1d.

Glennie, John Stuart, M.A.—
In the Morning Land. Containing precisely the same matter as "Isis and Osiris", now out of print. 3s. P. 6d.

Golden Library Series, The.—The Book of Clerical Anecdotes—Emerson's Letters and Social Aims—Godwin's (William) Lives of the Necromancers — Holmes' Autocrat of the Breakfast Table—Holmes' Professor at the Breakfast Table—Hood's Whims and Oddities, complete with all the original illustrations —Irving's (Washington) Tales of a Traveller; Ditto Tales of the Alhambra — Jesse's (Edward) Scenes and Occupations of Country Life—Leigh Hunt's Essays — Mallory's (Sir Thos.) Mort d'Arthur : the Stories of King Arthur and the Knights of the Round Table ; edited by B. Montgomery Rankin—Pope's Complete Poetical Works—Rochefoucauld's Maxims and Moral Reflections, with notes and introductory essay by Sainte-Beuve —St. Pierre's Paul and Virginia, and the Indian Cottage ; edited, with life, by the Rev. E. Clarke ; both series complete in one volume. Reduced to 1s. each, by post 3d. extra, or four can be sent by parcels post for 4s. 6d.

Goodwin, C. W., M.A.—
Story of Saneha. An Egyptian tale of 4000 years ago Published at 2s. 6d., post free.

Gospel History and Doctrinal Teaching Critically Examined, The. Cloth gilt, 255 pp., 2s. 6d. P. 4½d.

Groome, W., M.A., etc.—
Concise Tables for Chemical Analysis. Bound in limp cloth, Demy 8vo, 4d. **Post free.** Musical Harmony. 3d. P. 1d.

Gubernatis, Angelo de—
Zoological Mythology; or, the Legends of Animals. Two vols., 8vo, pp. xxvi. and 432, and vii. and 442, cloth (published at £1 8s.), reduced to 12s. 6d. Free by postal parcel, 13s. An important contribution to the study of the comparative mythology of the Indo-Germanic nations.

Half-Hours with Freethinkers—Shelley, Lord Bolingbroke, and Paine. The three post free 2d.

Hall, W. H. (Bullock)—
Gleanings in Ireland after the Land Acts. With map. Cloth 8vo, 115 pp., 1s. **P. 3d.**

Hamilton, C.—
Oriental Zigzag. Wanderings in Syria, Moab, Abyssinia, and Egypt. Handsomely illustrated. 304 pp., 2s. 6d. P. 4½d.

Hawley, J. H.—First Book of English Grammar. Cloth, 3d. P. 1d.

Health Lectures—
Defective Drainage as a Cause of Disease, by J. Makinson Fox; Clothing, by John Haddon, M.D.; Good Nursing and its Importance in the Treatment of Disease, by J. A. Irwin, M.D.; The House, by Henry Simpson. M.D.; Infant Feeding in Relation to Infant Mortality, by Henry Ashby, M.D.; Sick Nursing amongst the Poor, by C. J. Cullingworth. These Six Pamphlets containing invaluable information for the Prevention and Cure of Disease, will be sent post free for 7d.

Heine, H.—
Ludwig Börne. Recollections of a Revolutionist. Abridged and translated by T. S. Egan. 1s. P. 3d.

English Fragments, from the German. Translated by S. Norris. Cloth, 6d. P. 2½d.

Helps, Sir A.—Animals and their Masters. Cloth gilt, 220 pp. (published at 4s. 6d.), 1s. 6d. P. 3d.

Hill, S.—Egypt and Syria. 3s. P. 6d.

Hoare, E. N., M.A., Dean of Waterford—
Exotics; or, English words from Latin poets. Post 8vo, 334 pp., with thoroughly complete index, 1s. 6d. P. 4½d.

Holyoake, G. J.—
Child's reading book, 1d. The social means of promoting Temperance, with remarks on errors in its advocacy. Public lesson of the Hangman The three, post free, 3d.

Hogg, Jabez—
Elements of Experimental and Natural Philosophy. Being an Easy Introduction to the Study of Mechanics, Pneumatics,

Hydrostatics, Hydraulics, Acoustics, Optics, Caloric, Electricity, Voltaism, and Magnetism. 400 woodcuts, 560 pp. crown 8vo. (published at 5s.), 1s. 6d. P. 4½d.

Hone, W.—
The Apocryphal New Testament, being all the Gospels, Epistles. etc., attributed to Christ, his Apostles, and their companions in the first four centuries of the Christian era. 2s. 6d. P. 4½d.
Ancient Mysteries Described. With Engravings, 2s. 6d. P. 4½d.

Hughan, Samuel—Hereditary Peers and Hereditary Paupers : the two extremes of English Society. 152 pp., large 8vo, well printed and neatly bound, 1s. P. 3d.

Hugo, Victor, and Garibaldi—Political Poems. Post free, 1d.

Imperial Parliament Series—
Women's Suffrage. By Mrs. Ashton Dilke. With preface by W. Woodall, M.P., and
Leasehold Enfranchisement. By Henry Broadhurst, M.P., and Robert T. Reid, M.P. In uniform crown 8vo vols., bound in red cloth, 6d. each. P. 2d. The two post free, 1s. 3d.

Ingleby, C. M., M.A.—
Outlines of Theoretical Logic. Cloth, 88 pp., 6d. P. 1½d.

Jackson, Mrs. W. S.—
A Century of Dishonor ; a sketch of the United States Government's dealings with some of the North American Tribes. Cloth, 8vo, 457 pp. (published at 7s. 6d.), 2s. P. 4½d.

Kane, Sir Robert M.D., etc.,—
Elements of Chemistry, Theoretical and Practical, including the most recent discoveries and applications of the science to medicine and pharmacy, to agriculture, and to manufacture. Illustrated by 230 woodcuts, with copious index. Second edition. Cloth, royal 8vo, 1069 pp., 3s. 6d. P. 7½d.

Kant, Cousin's Philosophy of. With a Sketch of Kant's Life and Writings. By A. G. Henderson. 194 pp., neatly bound (published at 6s.), 2s. 6d. P. 4½d.

Kossuth, Louis—
Memories of my Exile. A complete history of the origin of the Italian War of 1859. Cloth, 446 pp., 2s. 6d. P. 4½d.

Laming, R.—
The Spirituality of Causation. A scientific hypothesis. Cloth gilt, 116 pp., 9d. P. 3d.

Lamon, W.—
Life of Abraham Lincoln. Portraits. Cloth, pp. 546. 5s. P. 7½d.

Latham, R. G.—
Russian and Turk. From a Geographical, Ethnological, and Historical point of view. Cloth, gilt, 434 pp. 3s. P. 6d.

Legge, Alfred Owen—
Growth of the Temporal Power of the Papacy. A historical review, with observations upon "The Council of the Vatican". Cloth, 8vo, 316 pp., 1s. 6d. P. 4½d.

Levi, Leone—Work and Pay. 3d. P. 1d.

Linton, Mrs. E. Lynn—
Witch Stories. A history of the witches of Scotland and England from 1479 to 1751. 320 pp., 1s. 6d. P. 3d.

Maccall, Wm.—Christian Legends of the Middle Ages. Cloth, 8vo, 320 pp., 1s. 6d. P. 4½d.

MacColl, Rev. M., M.A.—
Three years of the Eastern Question. Cloth, 8vo, 302 pp. (published at 5s.), 1s. 6d. P. 4½d.

Mackay, R. W., M.A.,—
Rise and progress of Christianity, cloth, 324 pp. (published at 10s. 6d.), 2s. 6d. P. 4½d.
The Eternal Gospel; or, the Idea of Christian Perfectibility. (Published at 2s. by Thomas Scott.) In two parts, 3d. each, in all, 6d. P. 2d.

Malan, Rev. S. C., D.D.—
Select Readings in the Greek Text of S. Matthew, lately published by Rev. Drs. Westcott and Hort. With a P.S. on "The Revisers and the Greek Text of the New Testament". 72 pp. in wrapper (published at 2s.) 3d. P. 1d.

Mansel, Professor—
Philosophy of the Conditioned : with criticisms on Mill's Examination of Sir W. Hamilton's Philosophy. 2s. P. 3d.

Manual, A Practical, of the Law of Sales of Food, Drinks, and Medicines, by a Barrister and Magistrate. Stiff paper cover, post 8vo, 80 pp. (published at 2s.), 3d. P. 1d.

McCosh, Rev. Prof. J., LL.D.—
The Association of Ideas, and its influence on the training of the Mind. 36 pp., wrapper, 1d. P. ½d.

Melancholy Anatomised. Showing its Causes, Consequences, and Cure. Also giving the definition, affection, matter, and species of melancholy, and dealing with love and religious melancholies. With anecdotal illustrations drawn from Ancient and Modern Sources. Founded chiefly on Burton's celebrated work. Crown 8vo, 300 pp., beautifully printed on toned paper, prettily bound, 1s. P. 3d.

Men of the Third Republic.—Cloth, 8vo, 384 pp., 1s. 6d. P. 4½d.

Mitra, Rajendralala, LL.D., C.I.E.—
Indo-Aryans: Contributions towards the Elucidation of their Ancient and Mediæval History.
Portion of Contents: Origin of Indian architecture—Principles of Indian temple architecture—Indian sculpture—Dress and ornament in ancient India—Furniture, domestic utensils, musical instruments, arms, horses and cars in ancient India—Beef in ancient India—Spirituous drinks in ancient India—A picnic in ancient India—On human sacrifice among the Athenians—On the Indian Styx and its ferriage—An imperial coronation in ancient India—On human sacrifices in ancient India—Funeral ceremony in ancient India—On the supposed identity of the Greeks with the Yavanas of the Sanskrit writers—On the Pála and the Sena dynasties of Bengal—On the peculiarities of the Gáthá dialect—On the

Rishya of the Aitareya Bráhmana—On the origin of the Hindi language and its relation to the Urdu dialect—Vestiges of the kings of Gwalior—Bhoja Rájá of Dhár and of his homonyms—Early life of As'oka—The primitive Aryans—Origin of the Sanskrit alphabet, etc.

Numerous illustrations, and very copious index. Cloth, new, uncut, 2 handsome vols., 8vo, (pub. at 36s.), 7s. 6d. P. 7½d.

MODERN REVIEW.—In good condition; 4d. per copy. P. 3d.

1882: January contains: Churches established and non-established, by Dr. G. Vance Smith; Herbert Spencer's Data of Ethics, by J. T. Bixby; Religious instruction in schools, by J. H. Smith; Richard Cobden, by S. Alfred Steinthal; Moral influence of the Christian pulpit, by J. Drummond, etc., etc. April contains: Ecclesiastes, by T Tyler; Materialism, by Mr. Justice Richmond; The seven Œcumenical Councils, by Dr. J. Hunt; Rhys Davids' Hibbert lectures; Jane Austen and Charlotte Brontë, by A. Armitt; Darwinism and religion, by H. W. Crosskey, etc., etc. 1883: January contains: The literature of Israel, by P. H. Wicksteed; Natural religion; Progress and poverty, by G. Sarson; Abolition of judicial oaths, by C. C. Coe, etc., etc. April contains: Catholic Church in France, by a French Catholic priest; Deuteronomy, by Prof. J. E. Carpenter; Overstrain in education, by R. A. Armstrong; Correspondence of Carlyle and Emerson; Man and his relatives: a question of morality, by A. Armitt; Memory and personal identity, by the Hon. Roden Noel, etc., etc.

Monteil, Edgar—Catéchisme d'un Libre Penseur. 1s. P. 3d.

Morley, John—
Diderot and the Encyclopædists, 8s. P. 4½d.
Rousseau. 2 vols. (published at 24s.), 7s. 6d. P. 7½d.

Motley, J. Lothrop (Author of "Dutch Republic")—
Democracy: the Climax of Political Progress and Destiny of Advanced Races. Demy 8vo, 32 pp., 2d. P. ½d.

Nayler, B. S.—The Sabbath question. 4to, 64 pp., 2d., post free 3d.

Nicholson, N. A., M.A, Trin. Coll., Oxon.—
The Science of Exchanges. 1s. P. 3d.

Nulty, A.—Land Agitation in Ireland. 2d.

O'Keefe, Father—
Ultramontanism v. civil and religious liberty. Demy 8vo, 270 pp., 1s. P. 4½d.

O'Kelly, E. de Pentheny—
Theology for the people. Cloth gilt, 9d. P. 3d.

Owen, Robert D.—
Lecture on Consistency. Situations—lawyers, clergy, physicians, men and women. 1d. each, post free.

Ozanam, A. Frédéric—
History of Civilisation in the fifth century. Translated from the French by ASHLEY C. GLYNN, B.A. 2 vols. in one, 470 pp., an excellent work, 2s. 6d. P. 4½d.

Paine, Thomas—
Political pamphlets—"Decline and fall of the English system of Finance"; "Letters to the citizens of America"; "Agrarian Justice opposed to Agrarian Law and Agrarian Monopoly, with a plan for creating a National Fund"; "Dissertations on the first principles of Government". The four free for 5d.

27

Paris, Comte de—
The Trades Unions of England. Translated by Nassau J. Senior.
Edited by Thomas Hughes, M.P. (Published at 7s. 6d.) 2s. P. 3d.

Parker, R. G., A.M.—
School Compendium of Natural and Experimental Philosophy
(published at 4s.), 1s. 6d. P. 3d.

Paton, A. A.—
A history of the Egyptian Revolution, from the period of the
Mamelukes to the death of Mohammed Ali. 2 vols., cloth,
published at 18s., now reduced to 5s. P. 7½d.

Peasant's Home, The.—Showing progress of agricultural laborers
from 1760 to 1865. Crown 8vo, 136 pp., 6d. P. 3d.

Poetic Treasures; or, passages from the Poets.—Chrono-
logically arranged from John Barbour and Geoffrey Chaucer in
the early part of the 14th century to Algernon Swinburne.
644 pp., 3s. 6d. P. 4½d.

POPULAR SCIENCE REVIEW.—(Illustrated by the best
Artists.) Only the following numbers now to be had. Price 3d.
per number (published at 2s. 6d.). **P. 3d.** The eight numbers
for 2s. 9d. Any five numbers free for 1s. 9d.

1879. January contains: Self-fertilisation of Plants, by Rev. G. Henslow;
Oldest Mountain in England, by C. Callaway; Electric Light, by W. H.
Stone; Origin of Tarns, by J. C. Ward; Gap between the Chalk and Eocene
in England and the Upper Cretaceous Floras, by J. S. Gardner, etc., with
illustrations. April contains: Evolution of the Elements by M. M. P. Muir;
Structure and Origin of the Limestones, by H. C. Sorby; Supposed New Crater
on the Moon, by E. Neison; Entomology, by W. S. Dallas; Sources and Uses of
Iron Pyrites, by J. A. Phillips, etc., with fine plates. July contains: The Birth,
Life and Death of a Storm, by Robert H. Scott; Extinct Animals of the Colonies
of Great Britain, by Prof. Richard Owen; The Silurian, Devonian, and Carboni-
ferous Rocks in the London Area, by R. Etheridge; Is Nest-building an Instinct
in Birds, by Benj. T. Lowne; Light-emitting Animals, by Prof. P. M. Duncan,
etc., most interesting plates. October contains: Geysers, Hot Springs, and Ter-
races of New Zealand, by J. Martin; Jade and Kindred Stones, by F. W. Rudler;
American Dredgings in the Caribbean Sea, by A. Agassiz; The Most Powerful
Telescope in Existence, by E. Neison; Flight and its Imitation, by Fred. W. Breary,
etc., illustrated.——1880. January contains: Law of Association in the Animal
Kingdom, by M. Edm. Perrier; Argentine Republic, by Chas. Oxlond; Meteors,
by W. F. Denning; The Dinosauria, by Prof. H. G. Seeley, etc., excellent plates.
April contains: The Threshold of Evolution, by Surgeon-Major Wallich; Arti-
ficial Diamonds, by F. W. Rudler; Chamæleons, by Prof. J. Reay Greene; The
New Chemistry, by M. M. P. Muir; Classification of the Tertiary Deposits, by
Prof. John W. Judd, etc., interesting illustrations. July contains: Climbing
Plants, by Francis Darwin; On the Influence of Electricity in the Formation of
Rocks, by M. F. de Castro; Feather Stars, Recent and Fossil, by P. H. Carpenter;
Sunspots and British Weather, by W. L. Dallas; Hardening and Tempering of
Steel, etc., beautiful plates. October contains: Opinions of Voltaire and Laplace
regarding Geology, by Prof. P. M. Duncan; A Large Crater, by Prof. John Milne;
Infusoria as Parasites, by W. S. Kent; The August Meteors, by W. F. Denning,
etc., with good illustrations.

Portraits—handsome, fit for framing, of John Bright, Gladstone,
and Beaconsfield, 6d. each.

Preston, S. Tolver—
Original Essays.—I. Social Relations of the Sexes; II. Science
and Sectarian Religion; III. Scientific Basis of Personal Responsibility; IV. Evolution and Female Education. Crown, 8vo,
80 pp., 6d. P. 2d.

Priestley, Joseph—The life and writings of. 1d.

Rae, W. Fraser—
Facts about Manitoba. Reprinted, with additions, from the *Times*. With two maps, 3d. P. 1½d. Useful to emigrants.

Ramage, C. T., LL.D.—
The Nooks and By-ways of Italy. Wanderings in search of its ancient remains and modern superstitions. Crown 8vo, cloth, 314 pp. (published at 10s. 6d.), 1s. 6d. P. 4½d.

Reade, Winwood—The Outcast, 1s. 6d. P. 3d.

Readings for Travellers.—4 vols. 6d. each. P. 1½d. Can be bought separately.

Reichenbach, O.—
Configuration of the Earth and the Evolution of its Mechanical Causes. 100 pp., 8vo, 3d. P. 2d.

Reid, Andrew—
The New Liberal Programme, contributed by Representatives of the Liberal Party. Containing Special Articles by Henry Labouchere, M.P.; Jacob Bright, M.P.; Thomas Burt, M.P.; Sir Wilfred Lawson, Bart., M.P.; and Twenty other Members. Cloth, 204 pp. Published at 2s. Reduced to 6d.

Robertson, J. (of Cupar-Angus)—
The Finding of the Book. An essay on the origin of the Dogma of Infallibility. This is the important work which provoked the famous heresy prosecution. Published at 2s. Post free 1s.

Roscoe, W.—
Life and Pontificate of Leo X. Neatly bound, pp. 425, 1s. P. 2½d.

Rossel, Capt. L. N.—
Posthumous papers. Including letters to Gambetta and others, 1871. Pp. 294. 1s. P. 3d.

S., C. V.—Letters to and from Rome in the years A.D. 61, 62, and 63. Translated. Cloth, 8vo, 69 pp., 6d. P. 2d.

Salamanca, Don Felix de—
The Philosophy of Handwriting. With fac-simile autographs of distinguished authors, artists, statesmen, journalists, etc., etc. Cloth, 8vo, 153 pp. (published at 4s. 6d.), price 1s. P. 3d.

Salvator of Austria, Archduke Ludwig—
Caravan route between Egypt and Syria. With 23 full-page illustrations by the author, demy 8vo, cloth extra (published at 7s. 6d.) 3s. P. 4½d.

Samson, G. W.—
The English Revisers' Greek Text shown to be unauthorised, except by Egyptian copies discarded by Greeks, and opposed to Historic Texts of all ages and churches. Paper, 132 pp., 6d. P. 2d.

Sane Patient—
Experiences in a lunatic asylum. Cloth, 167 pp., 1s. 6d. P 3d.

Sangster, J.—
Rights and duties of Property. Plan for paying off the National Debt. The Land Question. Cloth, 260 pp., 6d. P. 3d.

Satan : His existence disproved. 1d. P. ½d.

Scott, Thomas—
English Life of Jesus. Cloth, 349 pp. 2s. 6d. P. 4½d.

Scottish Border Minstrelsy (Collected by Sir Walter Scott)—
Half-calf, gilt. 3s. P. 4½d.

Shelley, P. B.—(The Poet of Atheism and Democracy.) Later Poems. 1s. P. 3d.

Simon, Collyns, Hon. LL.D.—
Solar Illumination of the Solar System. Cloth 8vo, 219 pp., 1s. P. 3½d.

Smith, Adam—
Inquiry into the Nature and Causes of the Wealth of Nations. Cloth 8vo, 780 pp., 2s. P. 4½d.

Smith, Arthur—
Political Economy Examined and Explained. Containing an explication of that which the public understand by the words wealth, value, and capital. Cloth gilt, 196 pp., 1s. P. 3d.

Smith, Sydney—
Essays. Reprinted from the *Edinburgh Review*, 1802 — 1818. Pp. 508, cloth 8vo, 2s. P. 4½d. Contains the famous essay against the Society for Suppression of Vice.

Sonnenschein, A.—
Educational Code Reform, being a compar'son between fifteen foreign codes and the English code. With a letter from A. J Mundella, M.P. 162 pp. Reduced to 3d., post free.

Stapleton, A. A.—
The Foreign policy of Great Britain, from 1790 to 1865. Demy 8vo, 300 pp. 2s. P. 4½d.

Survival, The, with an apology for Scepticism. 471 pp. 1s. P. 4½d.

Taine, H. A.—
History of English Literature. Translated by H. Van Laun. 2 vols. Vol. I. 530 pp. ; Vol. II. 550 pp. (published at 21s.) 12s. P. 7½d.

Taylor, Rev. Robert, B.A.—
The Devil's Pulpit : being Astronomico-Theological Discourses. Two vols. bound in one, 2s., originally published at 8s. P. 6d

Torrens, W. M., M.P.—
Marquess Wellesley ; Pro-Consul and Tribune. An historic portrait. 520 pp. Demy 8vo. (Published at 14s.) 2s. 6d. P. 6d.

Travis, Henry—Advanced Co-operation English Socialism, 2d. Manual of Social Science, 2d.

Trollope, T. A.—
    The Papal Conclaves, as they were and as they are. 434 pp., handsomely bound (published at 16s.), 3s. P. 6d.

Trial of P. McDouall, the Chartist. Post free, 2d.

Udny, Geo. (Barrister)—Harmony of Laws. 6d. P. 2d.

Unity, Duality, and Trinity of the Godhead.—With digressions on the Creation, Fall, Incarnation, Atonement, Resurrection, Infallibility of the Scriptures, Inspiration, Miracles, Future Punishments, Revision of the Bible, etc. A discussion by over 250 clergymen, Dissenting Ministers, and Laymen. Cloth, 8vo, 250 pp. (published at 6s.), 10d. Post free, parcels post, 1s.

Valbezen de, E.—
    The English and India. Origin and beginning of the Mutiny, siege of Delhi, siege of Lucknow, insurrection in Central India, cause of the Mutiny, end of the East India Company, the new charter for India, etc., etc. Cloth, 498 pp. 3s. (published at 12s.). P. 6d.

Van Laun, Henri—
    History of French Literature, from its origin to the end of Louis Phillippe. In 3 vols. New and uncut, 1244 pp. in all, 18s. (Published at 24s.)

Vign, Cornelius—
    Cetshwayo's Dutchman : private journal of a White Trader in Zululand during British Invasion. Notes by Bishop Colenso, and portrait of Cetshwayo. Cloth, gilt. 193 pp. 1s. 6d. P. 4½d.

Volney, C. F.—Lectures on History. Post free 6d.

Von Cotta, Prof. Bernhard—
    The Development-Law of the Earth. Cloth, 43 pp. Post free 6d.

Wake, C. Staniland—
    Chapters on Man, with the outlines of a Science of Comparative Psychology. Pp. 343 (published at 7s. 6d.), 2s. 6d. P. 4½d.

Wall, D.D., Charles William—
    Examination of the Ancient Orthography of the Jews and of the original state of the text of the Hebrew Bible. Part III., Vol. 1 : The sacred text originally written without vowel-letters or any other signs whatever of the vocal considered apart from the articulate, ingredient of syllabic sound. Cloth, crown 8vo, 376 pp., 2s. P. 4½d.

Walpole, Hon. Spencer—
    Life of the Right Hon. Spencer Perceval, including his correspondence with numerous distinguished persons. In 2 vols., cloth 8vo, with portrait, 3s. P. 7½d.

Wartegg, Chevalier de Hesse—
    Tunis; the Land and the People. Containing 22 very fine

engravings, handsomely bound in cloth gilt, pp. 292 (published at 9s.), offered at 2s. P. 6d.

Watson, Rev. J. S., M.A.—
Biographies of John Wilkes and William Cobbett, with steel engravings. Good index, 410 pp., 2s. 6d. P. 4½d.

WESTMINSTER REVIEW.—Religious, Political, and Social Questions, Science, Art, and Literature, dealt with by the ablest writers of the times. The following numbers can be obtained at 6d. each, and, besides the articles mentioned below, contain reviews of the contemporary literature. It will be better to buy several numbers, as they go very cheaply by Sutton or rail; and by post each 4½d. extra. By parcels post six numbers can be sent post free for 3s. 6d.

1867. April contains Italy and the War of 1866; Papal Drama; Thomas Hobbes; New America; Hopes and Fears of Reformers; Swinburne's Poetry; Contemporary Music and Musical Literature, etc.——1870. July contains Unpublished Letters of Samuel Taylor Coleridge, 1815-16; Indian Taxation; Future of the British Empire; Shelley; Roman Catholicism, Present and Future, etc. etc.——1871. July contains Religious Life and Tendencies in Scotland; Walt Whitman; Genesis of the Free Will Doctrine; Republicans of the Commonwealth; Early English Literature; Function of Physical Pain; Method of Political Economy, etc., etc. October contains Pilgrim Fathers; Greek Democracy; Faraday; Chaucer; Modern Science and Arts; Authorship of Junius; The Baptists; Leasing, etc., etc.——1874. April contains The Bible as interpreted by Mr. Arnold; Pangenesis; Song of Songs; Development of Psychology; Moral Philosophy at Cambridge, etc., etc.——1875. July contains Sunday and Lent; Allotropic Christianity; Education in Prussia and England; Evidences of Design in Nature, etc.——1876. July contains Sunday in England; Early Phases of Civilisation; Compulsory Medication of Prostitutes in England; Renan's Philosophical Dialogues; Lord Macaulay, etc., etc. October contains Political Economy as a Safeguard of Democracy; Indian Affairs; Lord Althorp and the First Reform Act; William Godwin, etc., etc.——1877. April contains Courtship and Marriage in France; Slavery in Africa; Russia; Charles Kingsley; Popular Fallacies concerning the Functions of Government, etc., etc. July contains Chartered Guilds of London; Illicit Commissions; Harriet Martineau; Our Gaelic Culture; Cradle of the Blue Nile; The Eastern Question, etc., etc.——1878. January contains Democracy in Europe; Education of Girls; their admissibility to Universities; The Indian Famine; Charles Sumner; Lessing; Charlotte Brontë, etc., etc. April contains Russian Aggression and the Duty of Europe; An Indian District; its People and Administration; Popular Buddhism according to the Chinese Canon; Peasant Life in France and Russia, etc., etc. ——1880. January contains Social Philosophy; Russia and Russian Reformers; Early Greek Thought; Colonial Aid in War Time, etc., etc. April contains Marquis Wellesley in India; Masson's Milton; Greek Humanists; Nature and Law; Charles Dickens; Animal Intelligence; India and our Colonial Empire, etc., etc.——1881. July contains George Eliot, her Life and Writings; Characteristics of Aristotle; Island Life; George the Fourth; Development of Religion, etc., etc.

Wikoff, Henry—The Four Civilisations of the World. 416 pp., cloth, reduced to 2s. P. 4½d.

Willis, R., M.D.—
Servetus and Calvin. Splendid portraits of Servetus and Calvin. Demy 8vo, 542 pp. (published at 16s.), 4s. P. 6d.

Yeats, J., LL.D., &c., and others—
The Natural History of Raw Materials of Commerce. A Manual of Recent and Existing Commerce from the year 1789 to 1872. The Technical History of Commerce. In six vols. (published at 18s.), 4s. 6d. By parcel post, 5s. 6d.

Yorke, Onslow—
   Secret History of "The International" Working Men's Asso-
   ciation. Crown 8vo, 166 pp, limp cloth (published at 2s.), 6d.
   P. 2d.

THE

National Reformer.

EDITED BY

CHARLES BRADLAUGH.

WEEKLY—PRICE TWOPENCE.

Post-free per annum to any part of Great Britain, Europe, Egypt,
the United States, and British America, 10s. 10d. New Zealand,
Australia, British African Colonies, South America, West Indies,
Ceylon, and China, *via* United States, 13s. India, Japan, and China,
via Brindisi, 15s. 2d.

OUR CORNER:

A MONTHLY MAGAZINE EDITED BY

ANNIE BESANT.

Containing articles and notes on Socialism each month, as well as
articles of general interest.

PRICE SIXPENCE, Post free, Sevenpence ; Yearly Subscription,
post free, Seven Shillings.

A. BONNER, Printer,

34, BOUVERIE STREET, FLEET STREET, E.C.

London : Printed by ANNIE BESANT and CHARLES BRADLAUGH,
63, Fleet Street, E.C.—Dec., 1887.

www.ingramcontent.com/pod-product-compliance
Lightning Source LLC
Chambersburg PA
CBHW031455270326
41930CB00007B/1006